DELUSIONAL RELATIONSHIPS

Truth or Fantasy

DELUSIONAL RELATIONSHIPS

How They Are Formed, How They Falter and Fail

AVERIL MARIE DOYLE

PRAEGER

Westport, Connecticut
London

Library of Congress Cataloging-in-Publication Data

Doyle, Averil Marie.
    Delusional relationships : how they are formed, how they falter
and fail / Averil Marie Doyle.
        p.   cm.
    Includes bibliographical references and index.
    ISBN 0–275–95010–7 (alk. paper)
    1. Interpersonal conflict. 2. Delusions. I. Title.
BF637.I48D69   1995
   158′.2—dc20   94–32926

British Library Cataloguing in Publication Data is available.

Library of Congress Catalog Card Number: 94–32926
ISBN: 0–275–95010–7

First published in 1995

Praeger Publishers, 88 Post Road West, Westport, CT 06881
An imprint of Greenwood Publishing Group, Inc.

Printed in the United States of America

The paper used in this book complies with the
Permanent Paper Standard issued by the National
Information Standards Organization (Z39.48–1984).

10 9 8 7 6 5 4 3 2

To the magic of truth

in relationships.

Contents

Illustrations

Preface

In the preparation of this volume, I have endeavored to present a collection of case studies or stories that illustrate the nature of delusional relationships. The process whereby these relationships are formed and then falter and fail, is considered in detail. Relationship reformation is also presented in such a manner that the process can be replicated, with or without professional assistance. Reformation is possible if the participants are willing to encounter the truth about themselves, their relationship counterparts, and the forces that shape their feelings, thoughts and behaviors.

The individuals, or personifications, presented in the studies represent conglomerative identities. For every person, couple, or family portrayed there are literally thousands of people in relationships that have presented therapists with similar, or even identical, problems. This sampling is not limited to the clinical population. Many of the people and life circumstances depicted on these pages can be found in the general population. Delusional relationships, and the individuals who participate in them, are everywhere. In every home and business, every school, hospital, or church, or in any other place where people come together to relate, there is delusion and misperception. This is the norm.

The language utilized throughout the volume is at times idiomatic and occasionally vulgar. It is the language of people in pain, who express themselves with words that are familiar and meaningful to them. To change that form and usage would rob the text of authenticity. Its inclusion serves another useful purpose for educators and mental health professionals: it desensitizes. When people speak of their innermost feelings, vulgarity is common. Four-letter words abound. In listening and counseling, acceptance is therapeutic. I have faithfully tried to represent individuals coping with delusional relationships. My intention is not to reproduce coarse language for sensational or shocking purposes, rather to portray the authentic human experience of those caught in delusional relationships, as I have witnessed it.

In compiling and presenting these case studies, the feelings and thoughts of individuals have been disclosed. A consistent effort has been made to establish the internal frame of reference of each relater. The structure of the individuals' thoughts has been depicted so that the reader can have access to their innermost emotions.

Pain is a necessary part of recovery, and there is no evading it. Delusionary thinking must be encountered, which necessitates the integration of severe disappointment. The fear of pain is exaggerated. The psychological experience involves anguish, shame, and the realization that one has been cruelly and unnecessarily out of touch with reality. The experience can include tears, visceral tension, facial tightening, the urge to vomit, chills, fever, and tachycardia, all followed by relaxation and a sense of relief and gladness. There is an accompanying rise of self esteem, an enhanced relating ability, and a pervasive sense of release and freedom. Encountering the pain associated with embracing truth is a healing experience. It dissipates delusion and illuminates reality.

Acknowledgments

I gratefully acknowledge:

Charles Francis Dorlac, my friend and editor, whose humor, insight, and steadfast support are greatly appreciated.

Diane and Douglas Alpert, whose friendship and thoughtful involvement added a needed dimension to this work.

Michael Mulhearn, whose generosity in providing his time and stimulating comments contributed immeasurably.

Elaine Darst, whose personal and professional reactions promoted insight.

Sharon Marie Doyle and Daniel William Doyle, whose participation as readers warmed my heart.

Tamar Marie Doyle, whose youthful perspective and openness provided freshness with amazing consistency.

Carolyn Harlan, who persevered through numerous editings of this work with strength and fortitude.

Roger Leonard Stockman, whose illustrations symbolize the concepts presented in this work. Stockman is an illustrator of children's books who has gained recognition for outstanding performance in the arts with particular notice given to his still-life drawings.

Introduction

At its core, a delusional relationship is dependent on a poorly organized network of information comprised of half-truths, misperceptions, and past experience. In the process of plying my trade, I have listened to thousands of people describe their feelings, attitudes, and behaviors. I have also witnessed their convoluted and tortured efforts to maintain delusion and avoid truth. This avoidance is not the result of cowardice, it is a normal and predictable human impulse to shield oneself from discomfort. Ironically, the dreaded discomfort provides the only sure exit to the dilemma. The experience of encountering truth can be as beautiful as it is uncomfortable. When the delusion fades, reality emerges. The core of the relationship is reformed, utilizing more accurate perceptions, which are based on the present rather than on past experience.

Regardless of the presenting problem, a persistent pattern emerges. People are generally unaware of the forces that have governed their thoughts, feelings, and behaviors. The choices they have made are more the product of social pressure than the result of conscious resolve. Their judgments about themselves and others have been determined by cultural injunctions, stereotypes, and symbols. In relationship formation, deluded thinking is the norm. This is true for everyone: delusional relationships are not limited to the clinical population.

As children, we are provided with limited role models: we see only those that are available in our immediate environments. These include only our parents, siblings, extended family, and perhaps a few neighbors. This is hardly enough to exemplify the richness of possibilities available to children for patterning human behavior and forming our identities.

There are numerous stereotypes for being a man or a woman and many different ways to be a spouse, parent, or child. Variation is possible in virtually every role available in any relationship. However, since our exposure to these models is limited and sometimes random, it is improbable that a good fit will magically occur. I see many mismatches--many cases of people forcing themselves into patterns or stereotypes for living that do not fit. Mismatches result in tension that is absorbed into the relationship and projected onto the relationship counterpart. If a male forces himself into a Tarzan stereotype in spite of the fact that he does not resemble Tarzan, he will strain to fit the role. This will be difficult and he will feel tension: it is a mismatch. Rather than abandon the stereotype, the would-be Tarzan looks around for Jane, as he is desperate for help in meeting his adopted stereotype. When he spots Jane--or a rough approximation of Jane--he will force her into the complementary role, thus compounding the mismatch. If this hapless male had been allowed to select an identity for himself more suited to his individual characteristics, he would undoubtedly have selected another type of woman who was more likely to fit as his counterpart. Poor Jane--she thought she was involved with Tarzan, someone who could help in her own search for identity. The experience is misleading and Jane discovers that she was sadly mistaken. What a mess: this is an example of a delusional relationship.

Most of us are as limited as Tarzan and Jane in the freedom we allow ourselves. If we were exposed at an early age to the many legitimate ways there are to be a man or woman, mismatches would be rare.

Helping troubled people reform their relationships has generated numerous questions in my mind regarding the cause of relationship failure. I have concluded that to improve our current educational system, it should be expanded to include sequential units of organized information on relationships, role taking, stereotypes, and cultural injunctions. Children in primary and secondary grades would benefit from a regular evaluation and assessment to clarify their level of understanding of these important concepts. Delusional thinking regarding relationships could thus be clarified and corrected.

Units on family relationships, dating and sexuality, marriage, parenting, and aging are viable modules for inclusion in the curriculum. Parents, churches, and social organizations are currently expected to provide this highly significant educational material. Unfortunately, they are not equal to the task. This is borne out by the high incidence of relationship disturbance and failure.

Knowledge that is generally classified as social psychology is relegated to an elective position in school curriculum. Information on attitudes and learning theory could be distilled and formed into level appropriate units. Education would be less like inoculation and indoctrination. Young learners who understand the process in which they are engaged will be active participants who are motivated to consolidate and expand their knowledge base.

The focus on core subjects such as reading, writing, and arithmetic has not yielded well-rounded individuals capable of understanding and participating in human relationships. Moreover, the exclusion of key information on living has rendered our educational system boring, irrelevant, and ineffective.

Through the years, I have listened to people berate themselves for turning out "just like Mom or Dad." They are overcome with anger and regret because they themselves are currently exhibiting behaviors, attitudes, and mannerisms that they despised in their parents and vowed never to incorporate into themselves. Given the principles of learning, particularly in regard to modeling and imitation, it is improbable that this type of learning could be totally avoided. Children naturally imitate the behaviors of those around them. It might be possible, however, to limit this type of behavioral transmission by raising the awareness of parents and children alike.

The process of learning is continual. All modeled behaviors are likely to be assimilated by the young learner. For example, a mother, Holly, has temper tantrums in front of her daughter, Joan, and Joan learns to have temper tantrums from watching her mother. Holly did not intend to transmit that behavior to her daughter, and Joan did not willingly choose to adopt temper tantrums as a coping mechanism. If, at an early age, however, both Holly and Joan had been educated about the process of learning, their awareness levels regarding the transmission of unintentional learning would have been heightened. Thus the possibility of avoiding unintentional learning would have been increased.

Education for living is effective. For example, recent efforts to educate children to resist sexual abuse look promising. The significant factor in this educational effort is simply raising the awareness of children regarding the dangers of sexual abuse and informing them that they have the choice to resist. Perhaps the same educational procedure can be adopted to alert learners at an early age about the various types of social learning pressures they will encounter throughout life. Children would thus learn about learning and the power of imitation and modeling. Education might even become a participatory venture, which would stand in sharp contrast to the passive learning that characterizes the existing system.

Delusional relationships are the direct result of ineffective education. People are unaware of the forces that determine their choices and behavior. With or without a change in our educational system, individuals trapped in delusional relationships need assistance. Generally, they are unable to release themselves from maladaptive patterns of relating until they gain insight into their misperceptions and false belief systems.

Joshua needed a woman who deferred to him. His first wife, Clara, had done this. Joshua consistently invoked biblical passages to bolster his position of male superiority in the relationship. Clara was good-natured and essentially ignored his hostile, deprecating attacks on women. The aggression was all verbal. Moreover, Joshua was a nice enough person "as long as the pussy was good." Whenever Clara resisted a sexual encounter, however, he made nasty remarks and withdrew. When Clara died, he had trouble replacing her and declared that "they don't make women like Clara anymore." The women he dated were attracted to Joshua at first but rapidly determined that he was more trouble than he was worth. One after another they stopped returning his calls. Joshua was angry. He felt that women no longer knew their place. His prior learning had conditioned him to expect deference just because he was male. When he received deference, he proceeded to push the stereotype by belittling the woman and building his ego at her expense. It was at this point that his relationships faltered and Joshua found himself alone again.

When Joshua presented himself for counseling, he had no insight into his own behaviors or the fact that he was operating from an outdated stereotype. Joshua was fifty-nine. He was uninterested in his age-mates. He wanted a younger woman, aged thirty-five to forty. He did not like fat women. He advertised through the personal ads for a petite, old-fashioned girl. Joshua lamented the effect of feminism on women, saying that all feminists deserved to be turned over some man's knee and spanked. As he talked, his inadequacy feelings became more pronounced. I asked him repeatedly if there was anything he was doing that discouraged his relationship prospects. My questions angered him, yet he returned, week after week, to talk about his ongoing difficulties in relationship formation. Joshua finally concluded he was better off alone. He would never find a woman who would accept him on his terms. He was right--Clara was the last of a dying breed.

Joshua could not adjust to the changes that had occurred in the nature of relationships and gender equality. He was unprepared for the current reality. He deluded himself that the pattern he had observed in his parent's marriage was still a viable one. Had he been exposed to other models for male-female relationships, he might have been able to risk a new relationship style. As it was, his counseling experience facilitated insight into the cultural changes that had rendered his current style obsolete. Joshua was not motivated to adopt a modern, less objectifying view of women, which he felt would detract from his own stature as a man. He preferred to suffer from loneliness rather than abandon his cherished stereotype.

There are many Joshuas: good men trying to live their lives as they were taught. Invariably they seek a complementary relationship counterpart to somehow complete them. This is little different from Cinderella waiting for Prince Charming, Barbie doll looking for her Ken, or Olive Oyle waiting for Popeye. One stereotype is dependent on another to maintain it. Vulnerability occurs when an individual is stereotype dependent and cannot function without the structure this provides. When one becomes typecast, not only is there a dependency on the stereotypic counterpart, but an overdependance on roles and scripts develops. In Joshua's case, rigid typecasting and role dependance resulted in confusion and anxiety when a crisis occurred. His wife died. The structure which supported his identity collapsed. Counseling increased his understanding of his situation, it is unclear, however, whether the insights he experienced would eventually be sufficient to promote adaptation.

Joshua's case demonstrates how delusional relationships limit freedom of expression and function as a barrier to authentic relating.

PART I

THE DELUSIONAL PROCESS

Chapter 1

Defining Delusional Relationships

Imagine being transported back in time to an early classroom setting. It is a little different than you remember. There is an aura of excitement and discovery. The purpose of school is explained clearly. You are given information about significant things in life, like how to understand yourself and how to relate to others. You learn about gender and sexuality, the meaning of being a boy or a girl, and the many choices you have, like whether or not to be a mom or dad, marry or remain single, relate to the same or opposite sex.

You learn about role taking and how to avoid being restricted by the expectations of others. You discover attraction, the force that affects your choices of friends and life mate. You learn how to form relationships and maintain them, how to acknowledge and express feelings. How to recognize differences as well as similarities. You learn how to make informed choices. You learn the difference between delusion and reality.

Nice little fantasy, isn't it? In reality, our educational experiences do not prepare us to understand ourselves or others. Nor are we provided with information on relationships and role taking. We are not made aware of cultural messages or the meaning of gender based restrictions and how they affect our lives. Consequently, most of us are involved in delusional relationships, relationships that are based in fantasy and misperception.

A delusionary or fantasy relationship is not real. A delusion is a false belief, especially a persistent false belief. Delusion is also defined as the state of being deluded or led astray. A fantasy is a belief unrestrained by reality, an unreal mental image.

Marlene's mother was fat.   Marlene was thirteen years old when she discovered what a liability that was. To have a fat mother meant you had to live in fear of getting fat yourself. Nothing could be worse: no one likes a fat woman. There would be no dates, few friends, and probably, no marriage. Until she was thirteen, Marlene had thought her mother was beautiful and enjoyed spending time together, doing "girl stuff," and going places with her.

It all started when she realized that the pretty women on television and in magazines were thin. Similarly, heroines in romance novels were never fat. There was also a continual association of being lazy with being fat. Fat women ate too much and didn't work or exercise enough. Men divorced fat wives or cheated on them with thinner women. It was a burden to have a fat mother. Marlene began to hate her mother, which made her feel guilty.

Joe's father was arthritic. He limped when he walked. When Joe was a toddler he began to walk the way his father did. When Joe began to grow up, by about the time he was age six or seven, he had learned there was something wrong with his father. Joe stopped limping, but his father never did. Joe continued to love his father, but he felt inferior, as if he, too, were arthritic. There was a strange feeling of loyalty in Joe that made him want to feel handicapped like his father.

These are misperceptions formed in childish minds, unknown and, therefore, uncorrected by parents and educators. They are representative of the normal thought process that we all experience. This process of association and overgeneralization results in misperception and forms the basis for delusional relationships.

This work will explore human fantasies and delusions--not the extreme kind that require hospitalization or medication, but common, everyday delusions and fantasies that we all subscribe to and perpetuate in our families and relationships.

Our relationships, whether by blood, marriage, or sexualized friendship, connect us to others, sometimes with bonds of mutual regard and affection and sometimes with mutual frustration and anger. The feelings we have and how we relate depends on what we expect from ourselves and others in our relationships.

The ideals we have for our relationships are often based on fantasy, delusion, and misperception. A delusion, meaning a fixed, false belief, is held in spite of evidence to the contrary. Although it is false, it is taken to be true. Now suppose we have that kind of false belief about what a parent, child, sibling, spouse, friend, or lover is supposed to be. We proceed to use the delusion as a measuring device to evaluate or judge those with whom we are relating. After constructing an unreal mental image, we impose it upon our relationship counterparts. An unreal mental image cannot be replicated in real life. So, you can see how expecting the impossible from self or others could cause problems in a relationship.

Let's look at parent-child relationships because we have all been children and see how they are formed. They are nonconsensual. Your child does not agree voluntarily to be in a relationship with you anymore that you agreed to be in a relationship with your parents. It just happens. A child quickly forms expectations of the parents, and expresses disappointment and impatience when the parent fails to meet those expectations.

Larry and Louise were devoted parents. They had two small children whom they both adored. They listened carefully to their children, making them feel very important. Frequently, Larry and Louise sacrificed their own needs for recreation and relaxation in favor of the needs of their children. The parents modeled unselfish behavior and they expected their children to absorb this value and return it in their relationship. This did not occur. Unwittingly, Larry and Louise had taught their children to be self centered and to expect more than their share of attention in their relationships.

Clearly, this is not the message the parents wished to impart. There are many factors that contribute to the learning process. We know this to be true in reading, writing, and arithmetic. Tests and other evaluation devices are utilized to illuminate the learning process as students advance from primary to secondary levels of education. No precise evaluation method has been applied to measure what children have learned about relating or about their the social identities. Self-knowledge is not considered a viable subject for consistent study and measurement in our current educational system.

Larry and Louise are not unusual parents. Rather, they are the norm. The messages intended for communication are diluted and misconstrued in the transmission process. Children misunderstand the messages and are frequently punished for this failure.

Parental ideas of what a child should be may, at times, conflict with ideas that the child has about his or her own identity. Children do not yield voluntarily to what is proposed by their parents. Parent-child relationships are nonconsensual, formed without any kind of agreement between the two parties as to what the relationship will be like or what rules will govern the behavior of the persons involved. Usually, the adult or parent prevails because the child is weaker and dependent upon the parent. As the child grows, a relationship struggle ensues in which the child attempts to wrest power from the parent, either giving or withholding love and affection as a bartering device. Children inflict pain and discomfort upon their parents as a way of obtaining more control or moving into a less dependent and powerless position in the relationship.

These bartering methods of withholding and giving love are carried over into other relationships formed later in life. Parents also give or withhold love as a way of obtaining relationship satisfaction.

When Charles was a little boy he had an older sister, a mother, an aunt, and a grandmother who paid a lot of attention to him. He learned how to act cute to promote their smiles and favors. He played peek-a-boo a lot. He had a lot of fun. It was his favorite time of life.

When Charles grew up he continued to act cute and expect a lot of attention. However, he did not always get it. Consequently, his feelings were hurt and he felt unloved. When he married, he expected his wife to be as attentive as the women in his family of origin had been. He misread his wife's behavior. When she failed to shower him with affection, he felt she was unloving and unresponsive. His misinterpretation of her inhibited his own responsivity. He gradually began to withdraw and withhold affection from her. All this occurred on a preconscious level. He never talked about it, so there was no way to clarify what was occurring.

When Lucy was a little girl, her father would give her a big kiss whenever she was good. If she did something to displease him, he would not kiss her. She valued the kisses, which came to symbolize approval. As she matured, she continued to have a positive association between kisses and approval. Sometimes as an adult, she had difficulty recognizing approval when it came without kisses. As a grown woman in the workplace, she was very dependent on external approval to feel competent. In her intimate adult relationships, she did not value kisses for their sensual and erotic value. They meant something else to her: external approval.

Vague, accidental linkings and mis-associations such as these occur on a regular basis during infancy, childhood, and adult life. Developing an awareness of these mis-associations would give parents and educators an opportunity to clarify and correct faulty learning before it could progress to a delusional stage.

Similar dynamics, rooted in mislearning, are found in consensual relationships. These are relationships that exist by mutual consent in which each party agrees voluntarily to form a relationship with the other person. Let's look at dating, romantic, sexual and marriage relationships. This type of relationship, ostensibly formed consensually, usually involves a certain degree of pretense on the part of both persons. Each presents as nicer, more understanding, and generous than they are likely to be as the relationship progresses. Each grooms him-or-herself in an attractive manner to promote interest and affection. There are countless variations in the initial phase of consensual relationship formation. Many of us do not focus on packaging ourselves attractively but inspire interest and promote affection by other means. We may smile a lot, be very helpful, or be especially attentive. There are many ways to make ourselves attractive to others. Newness carries its own excitement and by itself has the power to attract. As the relationship progresses, however, the tendency to present oneself favorably fades, as does the newness. The unfamiliarity, strangeness, and novelty wears off. It is at this juncture that we have the opportunity to see the person as he or she really is and to honor, learn to appreciate, and respect his or her uniqueness by familiarizing ourselves with his or her true characteristics. Unfortunately, it is also at this relationship juncture which likewise occurs in nonconsensual relationships that we most often falter and fail. People usually try to reimpose the fantasy, delusion, or stereotype.

Don was an eligible bachelor. At thirty-two, he really wanted to get married. All his male friends were married and many were fathers. He just could not find the right girl. He had been engaged twice and had been in three or four serious relationships with other women. He liked the feeling of being "in love" and the process of getting to know someone. He usually went through a similar process with each woman. He was playing a courting game rather than truly relating. He did not want to commit himself because when he did, he lost power in the relationship.

Both the women to whom he had been engaged had threatened to terminate of the relationship to secure an engagement ring. Don felt that he was taken for granted once the relationship reached the commitment stage. It was not until he expended the energy to learn how to relate beyond that point that he was able to successfully achieve his goal of marriage.

He had learned about courting, but not about commitment. The brief experiences provided by his church for engaged couples had been insufficient. They had not addressed salient points in depth. Don, like many other individuals, would have benefitted from ongoing education on relating, commitment and marriage long before he felt the social pressure to enter that phase of life. If he had understood more about the feeling of being in love-its purpose and its limitations-he would have felt less disillusioned and empty when the initial phase of attraction waned and subsequent stages of relating developed.

What actually occurs at this point? Let us return to the onset of a relationship and more closely examine the process of attraction more closely. In consensual relationships, physical appearance usually has a great deal to do with the initial attraction. Many of us have an ideal image of what constitutes beauty, whether male or female. This may be based on a family type. Frequently, we are attracted to others who look like our fathers or mothers--or the exact opposite of our fathers and mothers. However, it is amazing to me to observe how often people are attracted to someone who in some way resembles themselves. In attraction there may be a prominent feature or two that clearly or subtly resembles features of others we have loved or had strong feelings for in the past. Family resemblances, then, whether in facial type, body shape, or mannerisms can be a preconscious factor in initial attraction. Personality types or characteristics are also a component of initial attraction.

The way a person dresses, walks or smiles might catch our attention and interest. Now this is not very much to go on. The process of attraction is not very organized. These little glimpses or bits and pieces that we see do not really give us substantial information about the person. However, we will soon start "to fill in the blanks." This next step in the attraction process is even less organized and reliable. We start to construct a picture with fantasy and stereotypes, associating our past experiences and impressions with these bits and pieces of stimulus until we have created a very personalized and somewhat distorted perception of the object of attraction. This can happen in minutes, hours, or days, the time varies.

Generally speaking, this process occurs outside our awareness. The initial phase of attraction is the product of preconscious associations gleaned from our past experiences.

Other components of attraction in consensual relationships include wanting to be like the desired person in some way or to have what the desired person has, whether qualities, possessions, or status. But, the most significant aspect of the attraction process is that it is highly subjective, preconscious, and based on assumptions, projections, and stereotypes. These are not always an appropriate basis upon which to form a relationship. Let us look at a couple, Mark and Kelly, and the attraction process that drew them together.

They met at a party. Mark was attracted to Kelly because she had long blond hair and blue eyes. She looked a lot like the girls he had admired in high school but had never dated. He imagined she had been part of the "in" crowd, while he had not been. She wore a tight jean skirt that exposed a lot of thigh. Her "preppie" white blouse was unbuttoned to the third button, just the right amount to suggest accessibility.

Kelly really did not notice Mark at first. He was not very striking physically, but he had nice eyes and paid a lot of attention to her. She liked it that he seemed shy and was not as handsy as other boys she had dated. She was also pleasantly surprised when she discovered he drove a Porche, a cool car, and did not mind spending money on her. He took her to nice places, bought her sweat shirts and stuffed animals. She smiled a lot and made him feel smart and sophisticated by always deferring to him. She also gave him lots of oral sex and always seemed ready to be sexual. Kelly really responded to Mark. She did not need much foreplay, and she enjoyed it when Mark came. Sex was a big part of their initial attraction.

Mark reminded Kelly of her father, so she erroneously assumed he had qualities that her father possessed: stability, steadfastness, patience, and intelligence. As the relationship progressed, she also assumed that he would continue to work and produce sufficient income to support both of them so she would have the option of staying home or working part time like her mother did. Actually, Mark was very unlike Kelly's father and would have been amazed had he known that she saw him that way. He had never been a good student and had always had difficulty holding jobs--one of the many things Kelly did not know about him. He had failed to develop any interests other than constructing model airplanes, and of course he watched television the culturally designated sports events all males are supposed to like. Mark was not personally very interested in sports, but it was something to do and it was part of the male mystique.

Mark and Kelly did not focus on exchanging significant information about themselves. They just went through the dating routine. Mark was likewise uninformed about Kelly. He took her to be a strong, confident, independent woman who would be able to take care of herself and stabilize him. It never occurred to him that he would be expected to take on the role of major provider and protector. He felt more like a boy looking for a mother--a sexy mother, who would attend to all his needs and keep him on track. Mark was disappointed to learn that Kelly was not all that sexy. She had only appeared to be during the first phase of their relationship when she was in the role of a female attracting a male. Of course, he had engaged in all the complementary cues that evoked a sexual response in her. However, as the newness wore off and Kelly began to see Mark as he really was, an unformed male desperately seeking external support to fulfill the masculine stereotype, her sexual interest waned. He bored her. He was not a good conversationalist, primarily because he had no interests. His social skills were limited to superficial role behavior. How had she ever been interested in him?

Kelly's behavior had also been superficial. Her display of sexual interest and deference had been based on female role behavior that she knew would attract males. Those characteristics were dependent upon external cues. When she realized that Mark did not meet the male stereotype, she lost interest in nurturing him. She did not want to mother a young boy, she wanted to nurture and comfort an adult warrior home from hunting bear.

Neither party had been intent on deception, but deception had occurred. The forces of attraction, supported by role behavior and stereotypic thinking, had formed a delusionary relationship. False assumptions and misperception produced an aura of relationship mystique. Mark and Kelly never encountered each other as real people. They had no way of knowing whether there was a basis for authentic relating. They parted quickly as the delusion faded.

Fortunately, attraction does not always result in relationship establishment. Sometimes we are attracted and our interest is piqued but contact is not made and no relationship is formed. The recurrence of the attraction phenomena, however, does serve as a reinforcement of the pattern itself. Since there is no contact and no exploration of how realistic our assumptions are, we never discover or learn that the ideal image is a delusion or fantasy. Instead, we continue to have interest or attraction reactions to the same cluster of visual and personality characteristics.

After a relationship is formed and the delusion fades, people sometimes begin to panic and apply pressure to force themselves and their relationship counterparts back into the delusion or stereotype. This is an attempt to avoid confronting the reality of the situation and the actual person that is emerging from the delusion.

The attempt to reimpose the stereotype can be very painful, and even brutal. The point here is that this is not usually done with evil intent. Each person is truly desperate to maintain the fantasy, and the only way that can happen is to force the other person to play the part.

Scott was an average male. He was minimally confident in his relationship abilities. For that reason he relied heavily on stereotypes and role prescriptions as guidelines in his relationships with women. He usually paid for everything on dates and remembered to open doors and to lift and carry heavy things for his women. In return, he expected deference and some kind of token acknowledgment of his superiority. This expectation functioned at a preconscious level.

When he met Catherine, he liked her strong will and confidence. It made him feel especially good when she deferred to him, which she did, asking him for directions on how to get places and soliciting his opinion on matters of politics and sports.

As their relationship progressed, it became clear that Catherine was earning higher grades in the college classes they both attended even in math and chemistry, subjects in which males were supposed to excel. Scott became aware of a growing discomfort and shame because he could not successfully compete with Catherine. He usually earned C's. She was in the high B or A category.

He developed the habit of discounting her by making fun of her because she wore glasses. He also made comments about dumb blondes and how good they were in bed compared to the "schoolteacher types." Whenever Catherine had a big test to study for or an important paper to hand in, he tried to divert her attention from studying to sexualize with him. They had developed the pattern of having sex whenever he wanted it but only occasionally when she initiated or asked for it. It was a way for him to feel power--the power of being stereotypically male. He put her down to make himself feel powerful. He was able to do this because she was somewhat traditional and felt it was important to please her male.

As time went on, however, Catherine felt stifled by Scott's efforts to keep her in a subservient position. She began to see his put-downs as a sign of his inferiority feelings and lost interest in relating to him. Scott's efforts to maintain the illusion of male superiority had failed. Had he abandoned the stereotype and validated Catherine's strengths, the couple might have been able to develop a mutually satisfying relationship.

There are many other examples of stereotypic expectations that create relationship disturbance. A person in a romantic relationship, noticing that his or her counterpart is not smiling or acting happy, might demand or request a smile or make a remark such as, "It's not much fun around here anymore." Usually, little attention is paid to the cause of the unhappiness; rather, the unsmiling or unhappy person is given the message "if life's not fun, I'm outta here." This is a frequent occurrence; people of both sexes, in both consensual and nonconsensual relationships, tend to avoid unhappiness and expect a depressed partner to handle it privately and hide his or her true feelings.

In general, women are expected to smile more than men and to carry the burden of keeping everyone else happy. However, men also receive messages that tell them, "You are responsible for the happiness of your woman. If she's not happy, it's your fault." Most men accept responsibility for keeping their woman satisfied sexually. But women, in turn, are encouraged to express satisfaction to the point of faking organism so men will not feel inadequate. Many sexual relationships are less than genuine. Because of our sex negative society, people are afraid to talk about sex.

Nancy didn't want to hurt Jake's feelings. But she was dissatisfied with their sexual relationship. Since he had turned forty he was having trouble with erections. At first this had not bothered her because she thought it was temporary. Months went by without her mentioning it. Nothing changed except that Jake never attempted to have intercourse with her. Instead, he gave her oral sex or stimulated her manually.

She felt unfulfilled sexually and began to suspect he was being sexual with someone else. Whenever she tried to talk about it, he would curtly answer her questions and then fall silent. Her imagination began to race. She wondered if he had a sexually transmitted disease and was unwilling to tell her about it or if he was turned off by the signs of aging she was beginning to show. She gave up trying to talk to him about it, expressing her frustration by refusing any kind of sexual touch from him.

Jake felt rejected. He had a deep feeling of shame because of his erectile dysfunction. He did not want to talk about his feelings with Nancy, fearing he would be overcome with emotion if he did so. This would make him feel even less masculine.

Nancy finally left Jake, not because he had an erectile dysfunction, but because he would not talk about it with her. Nancy tried to hide her feelings, but she could not make it work. She could not maintain the delusion that everything was okay.

If Jake could have overcome his fears and talked about the problem or sought marital therapy, they probably could have selected one of the many constructive options available to men who develop erectile dysfunctions. Once again, lack of knowledge and overgeneralized fear resulted in relationship failure. Rather than seeking a workable compromise, Nancy and Jake abandoned their relationship when they could not force it into the stereotype.

Another example of reimposing a stereotype occurs when one member of a relationship starts acting nicer again, perhaps by preparing a special dinner with candles and music or appearing in a sexy outfit wearing cologne to generate interest and attraction. Frequently, flowers appear when a stereotype has been shattered. Flowers are a universal symbol of romance. When romance is fading, symbols can be used to reinstate the fantasy. The use of romantic symbols can be positive or negative, depending on the status of the relationship. If the relationship is totally dependent upon a romantic illusion, it cannot be sustained. Moreover, if romantic symbols are used as pressure to force a relationship counterpart into stereotypic behavior that does not fit, it is a futile gesture. Romantic symbols can be used positively to express playfulness, tenderness, and affection. Romantic symbols do play a large part in the formation of a consensual relationship. They also are commonly evoked to reimpose stereotypes and force conformity on a relationship counterpart.

Ask yourself if you are currently forcing yourself or another person into a stereotype.

Let's look at how stereotype imposition works in nonconsensual relationships. Think about your family homes, family gatherings and family reunions. These are times and places where we are expected to take certain roles, play certain parts, and perhaps give up other parts of our identity to maintain the overall stereotypic picture of the family. Ask yourself if, when you are with your parents, you regress and take on the behaviors of a child. Do you do this automatically? Does it occur by free choice or is it a response to pressure from your parents or other family members? Children frequently force their mothers into being the "good mom"--asking that they bake cookies, sew on buttons, decorate the house, or engage in other time honored behaviors that mothers are expected to enjoy. Children frequently encourage their parents to stay together in an unhappy marriage to maintain the delusion of a happy family.

Fathers are expected to be providers long after their children can provide for themselves. Aging parents are frequently pressured into making sacrifices to provide for grown children who should be totally self sufficient. The pressure applied to force parents back into the role of provider can create relationship resentment and disturbance. It also limits the development of a broader basis for relating. These types of familial exchanges are essentially one-way, with the parent giving and the child receiving. This is the norm when children are infants or very young and are unable to provide for themselves, but as the child matures, the provider role should diminish and exchanges should become more equal. It is often at this point in the parent-child relationship that role strain occurs. Frequently, the child has experienced the parent only as a provider and caregiver and there has been little or no focus on developing mutual interests or reciprocity. The parental role requires interest and support in the child's activities. Children, however, are not as consistently expected to show interest and support in the activities of their parents. This contributes to the one-dimensional nature of the parent-child relationship and is, undoubtedly, a major cause of relationship disturbance between adult children and their parents.

Role taking gives structure to our lives. Individuals need structure, to varying degrees. For the most part, however, role taking is difficult and damaging as it diminishes the uniqueness of each person. Role taking varies throughout the life span. We progress from being a child to a mate, parent, or autonomous adult. When we grow old, there is no role. Once again, our culture misleads us. The myth that we will be respected for our wisdom and experience, loved by our children, and taken care of as we weaken and falter can be another delusion. Let's look at Clyde, an aging parent.

Clyde was sixty-nine--an old sixty-nine. He walked slowly and rather stiffly as a result of an accident and subsequent back surgery. The worst time of his life had been when he was laid up in the hospital after the operation on his back. He had tubes, catheters, IVs, and almost unbearable pain. No one respected his privacy and he was treated like a child by the doctors and nurses. This infuriated him. It was as if he had no identity. Clyde had a graduate degree in engineering. During his life he had been a respected and productive scientist. He had made a great deal of money. He had taken the role of husband and father willingly and had done very well as far as he was concerned. Both his children had graduated from college. He had paid their way, including outrageous sorority and fraternity fees.

Today, however, he was sick and alone. Neither his daughter or his son had spent much time with him: one visit each. The obligatory visit. He got the impression they were waiting for him to die so they could inherit his money, pay off their mortgages and take trips to Europe. He did not tell them how he felt, of course--what good would it do? Just make everyone uncomfortable. He did not really want to see them anyway since he had to hide his feelings and pretend everything was all right.

Lorraine, his daughter, was preoccupied with her own loss. Her father was dying, or so she feared. His beautiful blue eyes looked so watery now. He was becoming deaf and he could hardly hear what anyone was saying. She was glad her mother was already dead so she could not see how bad it was. He wasn't a man anymore--just an old, worn-out shell. She wanted her father back. She felt old herself. With both her parents gone, or nearly gone, she could no longer delude herself that she was young.

She hated to go see him. What could she say? If she told him how she felt she would start to cry, and that would not work. So she stayed away--waiting for him to die or, maybe, he would get better so she would not have to worry about it for a while.

Tyler, his son, was truly shaken by his father's deterioration. He had always been so competent, so indestructible through the years, no matter what happened. His body now looked so small, so frail--like a woman's body. There was not any muscle left. No competitive hardness. The most difficult part was that sometimes it looked like he was almost crying. His father crying? This just did not fit. If that was what aging meant, Tyler wanted to die young, maybe in an accident or anything, just to avoid going through that.

It was painful to be around his father. Tyler did not know what to say. He could not cry and he did not want his father to know how he felt. It was too embarrassing for everyone. Best to remain silent. Maybe he would hug him. But that would feel strange. There had been so little touch between them except when he had been a child. His Dad used to hold him back then.

Clyde felt empty and alone. He had reached a time in his life when there were no more roles. No one knew him and no one wanted to know him. Did he exist at all? He was surprised--he had not expected this. He had done everything right, followed the rules, yet in return for all his efforts, he had nothing. He had no relationships and was too old and tired to form new ones. He was bereft of delusions and expectations.

Clyde had depended on roles to structure his life, to give him meaning and purpose. His self-esteem had depended on how well he filled his roles, but there are no roles for the aging and retired--no purpose. The culture no longer needed to control Clyde, so he was forgotten. He felt worthless, unloved, and unneeded.

Do you know Clyde, or someone like him, whose role dependency has hampered the development of authentic relationship skills?

Role strain is a very common cause of relationship disturbance and failure in families. It occurs when meeting expectations forced on us by our relationship counterparts becomes uncomfortable. Role strain also occurs when the role bearer becomes confused by conflicting messages from the culture in general. When a role bearer has endeavored to meet the cultural prescription and has not been rewarded for it, role rebellion occurs. The role bearer abandons the role. Myth perpetuation regarding the importance of the role is no longer powerful enough to bind the role bearer. We all participate in the perpetuation of myths in an effort to bind ourselves and others to unrewarding roles.

Let's look at a progression of messages that comprise a "mother-myth" for one boy, Tony. His initial memories and messages were associated with food. Mother made breakfast, lunch, and dinner and often supplied cookies and other snacks between meals. Tony's mother, Alice, was a good cook. His father, sister, and he all really enjoyed the products of her labors in the kitchen. He remembered with bitterness when her cooking began to taper off until finally she was not cooking at all. He, and the other members of the family, were indignant when she suggested they all take turns procuring food by shopping for groceries and preparing meals. Moms were supposed to do that! When she got her job and began to talk about going back to school for a degree, things really got bad at home. Tony felt like he did not have a Mom anymore. He was ashamed that she could not be Den Mother for Cub Scouts. "You're selfish," he had said, joining in on one of many family arguments in which everyone tried to tell Alice how she was harming them by changing her interests and life-style from a stay-at-home mom to a working mother going to school.

Tony got used to the changes, but he never forgave her. In fact, whenever she did anything for him, like making his bed or cleaning his room, he made a point not to thank her. He wanted her to know he was still mad. He wanted her to feel guilty and she did.

At first it bothered Alice a lot, and then she came to see that Tony did not love or accept her. He wanted a fantasy mom. What he knew about her as a real person, he apparently did not like. She cried, grieved, and gradually became bitter. Becoming a mother had been a mistake. No one, not even her husband, had ever acknowledged or thanked her for what she had done. It was only when she stopped doing it that they gave any indication it had been worthwhile or important.

Tony was her biggest disappointment. She had wanted him so much and loved him so dearly. She enjoyed taking care of him. He seemed to adore her and wanted to be with her all the time. When he was an infant, Alice would do her housework while Tony was asleep so she could spend time with him when he got up from his nap. She got her first inkling of the discounting she was to receive when Tony started choosing his father, Mac, over her whenever there was a choice. She knew it was natural for him to want to be with Dad and do "guy" things. Beside, Dad was not around as much as she was, so being with him was a novelty. As time progressed, however, Tony became less respectful and began to denigrate her because she was a woman. She had taught him to drive and even loaned him her car, which his father would not do that because he did not trust Tony with his own car. Alice had never gotten a traffic ticket or had a violation of any kind on her driving record. Soon after Tony got his learner's permit, he started making disparaging remarks about women drivers and took on a chauvinistic attitude toward Alice when they were together in her car. He had picked up some of that from his father, who also joked about women drivers.

Alice began to enjoy her son's company less and less until she avoided being with him and lost interest in providing him with gestures of love and comfort. "He changed from a sweet, loving child into a junior version of the Archie Bunker character. I've lost my little boy and in his place I have a rude, smart-mouthed, overbearing male."

As for Tony, he wondered what had become of his sweet, accepting mother who used to praise his accomplishments and smile at him in encouragement. He missed her and he wanted her back. He did not understand what had happened. Above all, he could not figure out why she was upset with him. All he wanted was a "normal" mom so that he could be a "normal" boy. Why should she be disappointed with her family? What did she expect?

Alice did have unmet expectations. She had married and had children because she thought it was her only option to be a good woman. She expected that in return she would be loved and appreciated. The myth promised her a position of respect in the eyes of her family and the community for having done the right thing. Instead, she was taken for granted, discounted, and ignored. Moreover, even though her family members were neither mean nor violent, she was emotionally abused. When she tried to do anything for herself, they labeled her as selfish. She vacillated between feeling cheated and foolish for believing the myths and feeling like a failure because she could not make the myth work for herself and her family.

Tony's feelings about his role as a son were just as confused. Was he supposed to mother her? He had noticed the look on her face when she felt left out. Was it his fault or did she just want too much? He remembered one time when, on her birthday, he found her crying in the garage because no one had done anything special for her. He had known something was wrong all day.

Even though they gave her flowers, no one had gotten her a cake or given her a party--something she always did for them on their birthdays. She did not say anything when he and Dad went out to the ball game, but later, in the garage, he saw her tears and felt her unspoken anger. Should he have baked her a cake? Should they have stayed home and celebrated with her? Moms were not supposed to need that. Boys grew up to have wives who did all that stuff for them. Girls just grew up to be wives and mothers and they were supposed to either like it or fake it. What had gone wrong? Was his mom just selfish?

What do you think? Was Alice selfish? Were Tony's expectations and reactions similar to those you might have had?

Stereotyping also serves a functional basis. It helps us process information and establish a view of the world. Stereotypes provide guidelines for our behavior when we do not know how to act. We live in a complex society and have to simplify an endless flow of information by reducing it to manageable segments. But this process of categorizing also limits and, therefore, distorts perceptions by creating categories of people based on a single factor, like women or men, parents or children, boyfriend or girlfriend, grandparent or grandchild. These categories limit our perceptions of people as individuals.

We then begin to construct a set of beliefs about the personal attributes of each of these categories. Half truths and overgeneralizations predominate. Men are unfaithful. Women are bossy. Grandparents love to babysit and spoil their grandchildren. Loving adult children always attend family gatherings and come home for Thanksgiving. These beliefs, whether negative or positive, promote expectations of these group members.

Another effect of this process is what we call the cognitive confirmation effect. This occurs when we become blinded to behaviors that do not fit the stereotypic categories we have constructed. We see and experience only what we believe to exist. and we screen out everything else. Thus delusion or fantasy may continue to exist despite voluminous evidence to the contrary. We see what we expect to see. We blind ourselves to behaviors that do not fit the stereotype. As the relationship continues, we adjust our own behaviors to fit the stereotype rather than the real person to whom we are relating. The process comes full circle. We become prisoners of the stereotypic counterpart. If an adult child forces the parent back into the role of provider, the adult child must remain a dependent child, which becomes the primary existing bond between parent and child.

As children, we form stereotypes and beliefs about what to do and expect in relationships. As mature adults, we are still controlled by them. Adults rarely escape the impact of relationship stereotypes formed in childhood. These patterns cause role strain or relationship disturbance throughout our lives. They form the basis for delusional relationships.

Maze: Appreciative or Resentful

Chapter 2

Role Taking, Gender-based Restrictions, and Gender-based Expectations

You are suspended in a giant web. The web is constructed of thousands and thousands of silken strands that stretch endlessly back and forth through time. The silken strands reach longitudinally as well as laterally. You are supported and guided by the web. There are indications regarding how to proceed and how to retreat. The glistening strands are gender specific. Males follow countless strands that help develop the characteristics needed to play their parts in the world. Females are restricted to other strands that develop another set of qualities needed to play their parts. The shimmering web can be quite helpful, even seductive, helping you find the easiest way. Perhaps it restrains, but it also prevents capricious movements which might damage you. It is helpful for some but harmful for others. Can you see and feel the silken strands? Are you appreciative or resentful of the web?

Our options are affected by our gender. Most of us do not like restrictions. We may rationalize and accept them as optional, gender-specific guidelines about how to look and feel. On occasion we can also select gender-neutral guidelines. There are fewer of these. Gender-neutrality is a new concept. It is evocative of freedom and choice: fewer restrictions, but perhaps more risk. There is always more risk when we leave the beaten path. Gender-specific systems are usually so pronounced and refined that laws and customs exist for the sole purpose of maintaining them, even if they no longer serve their original propose. Restrictions and expectations about what is acceptable, proper, and necessary to fill certain roles are communicated to us with regularity, sometimes subtly and sometimes with blatant insistence. Let's look at a simple custom and how it affected the lives of two people, Pearl and Cliff.

Pearl was a tomboy. She enjoyed sports of all kinds. She was fast, strong, and physically disciplined. She had good hand eye coordination. Pearl exemplified the perfect athlete. She was tall, very tall-six and a half feet tall. Females are not expected to be that tall; it doesn't fit the guidelines. When she was in grade school, she could not use an ordinary desk, which was too small. She had to sit at the front of her class at a separate table. She felt humiliated; she wanted desperately to look and be like everyone else, but her height made her different. Pearl was well liked for her quick smile and friendly manner. Sometimes she made jokes about her height to avoid anyone else commenting on it.

When she was twelve, Pearl started developing secondary sex characteristics. She had a beautiful body--beautiful but oversized. Her face was pretty, with creamy skin and large blue eyes. Her hair was long and curly, and she braided it. If she had been a foot shorter, she probably would have been sought after as a beauty queen. But her male peers were shorter and less developed than she, and they were very conscious of wanting to be taller and stronger than the girls they dated. Pearl did not meet the expectations that were presumed appropriate for a girlfriend. No one asked her out. She was heterosexual and had no interest in lesbian contact. But because of her size and perhaps, her athletic ability, she was not granted access to normal cross-gender sexuality.

In time, after a period of limited social and asexual existence, during which she neither masturbated nor related sexually to males, she drifted into the lesbian community. She was nineteen when she had her first lesbian sexual encounter. She did not enjoy sex with women, but felt compelled to play the part or act as if she were sexually aroused in order to fit into the community. There were other aspects of the gay community that disturbed her. Its minority status bothered her most. She already felt like an outcast; being a lesbian made it worse.

She was showing signs of depression when she first entered therapy. She no longer enjoyed working out or participating in sporting events. She was losing weight, had trouble sleeping, and could not concentrate. She felt worthless because she was not able to assume the roles normally available to a woman of her age. Guilt feelings regarding her participation in the gay community sometimes reached unbearable proportions. "It's so unfair to the women I'm with; I'm using them and cheating them. They think I'm a lesbian. I'm just hiding out in their community. I'm not even bisexual," she added, "but most of the community classifies me as a dyke woman. I'm so angry at men for rejecting me that even if one came along that wanted me, I wouldn't go for it. I couldn't trust him." She had been severely damaged by the combination of beliefs and circumstances that denied her normal sexual expression. Moreover, she had always felt discriminated against professionally and had trouble finding a position as a coach and exercise physiologist because of her size, which she was told, was intimidating. People of both sexes felt uneasy in her presence. Her height distracted from all other considerations of her, professionally or personally. She felt like a freak.

Becoming a member of the lesbian community further limited her in the mainstream culture. The time she spent there prevented her from finding a niche in heterosexual society. She started having dreams about cutting off her head so she would be shorter. I recommended medication, but she declined on the basis that it would have deleterious effects on her health. She seemed to draw comfort from talking about her feelings over and over again. She expressed herself repetitively. I listened without confronting her about the repetition. It served a useful purpose; ventilating her feelings, and clarifying her thoughts. Because of her height and her athletic inclinations, she did not fit the cookie cutter image of what a girlfriend, wife, and mother should be. She longed to fulfill these stereotypic roles. For her, this would symbolize acceptance and normality.

"I feel just like any other woman feels. I just don't look like one." Actually, she did look like most women, with one major exception; she was a foot and a half taller, her shoulders were a little broader, and her overall musculature was more obvious than that of the average woman. There were probably men who would be attracted to her if she waited long enough, but Pearl felt panic. Role strain diminished her ability to adapt and cope with her environment. After having been repeatedly ignored and rejected as a candidate for feminine roles, she internalized the rejection and began to see herself as ugly, undesirable, and unworthy. She was caught in her own cultural bias. She knew she did not fit the visual stereotype; even though she had a pretty face and a nice body, she was too tall for the feminine stereotype. Her world seemed bleak.

By the time she was a junior in college, she had become extremely bitter. "I'm handicapped," she said "Guys are admired if they're tall. They gain recognition and accolades for excelling in sports. But I get penalized for it."

There was no denying her plight. I did not comfort her with reassurance that someday a tall, enlightened male would appear and claim her as his own. The odds were against it, partially because she was developing an unpleasant personality. Silence and withdrawal characterized her demeanor, and her anger was fueling her depression.

Our focus in counseling was limited to her presenting problem: managing her feelings. Pearl also relied heavily on the support she received from the lesbian community. However, the support also increased her guilt. The women she met there all liked, admired, and respected her. Many were attracted to her sexually. It made her feel good to be wanted, but she could not share the arousal feelings. She was uncertain about resolving this issue. Her relationships with women were not very sexual. She involved herself in a lesbian encounter once every two or three months. As the guilt became more intense, she discontinued the physical component of her relationships with women.

"I'm still attracted to men. In fact, there's a guy at work who seems to like me, but I'm probably just imagining it." She was conflicted about even talking about the possibility. "I feel like a high school girl, he bought me a Coke and I'm building it up to be something it's probably not." I said nothing, hoping she was not due for another disappointment. I encouraged her to explore at a deeper level: "Talk about your fear."

It was hard for her to admit she was afraid. It did not fit with her view of how an athlete should feel, but she let herself cry silently and then went on to describe her fear that she was totally unattractive to this male, that he could not be interested in her as a woman and that he would be amused if he knew how she felt. She fell silent and asked what time it was. The exploration of her feelings was becoming uncomfortable. Maintaining the focus on her feelings, I asked her if she thought he would laugh, forcing her deeper into the pain.

She said "Yes" in a hoarse whisper. "Shame, I feel shame." I became aware of an undercurrent in my own response: surprise that Pearl was responding like a stereotypic woman. Was it the tug of my own cultural inoculation? Why should I be surprised if Pearl had normal feelings? Was I affected by a bias similar to the one Pearl had encountered from others in the society in which we both lived? She did not look like a normal woman, so she could not feel like one. A wave of uncertainty overwhelmed me. Had I colluded in Pearl's misperception of herself as unattractive and undesirable? I recalled my record of her treatment process, searching for signs of bias. Had I been too understanding when she drifted into the lesbian community? Would I have facilitated a deeper exploration of her options as a heterosexual if she more closely approximated the feminine stereotype? Mercifully, I concluded that the therapy had been sound and unbiased, but henceforth, I was acutely aware of how easy and how predictable it would be for me to reflect the bias of the general culture, of which I was a product. In spite of my training and experience, my reactions could be tainted by the enculturation process. I made a note to focus on the imposition of gender-based values in my training sessions, both for myself and my training associates.

Throughout my work with Pearl, I made a point to check my responses to her reactions. I did not limit her because she was striving to fulfill a stereotype that might be as restrictive as the one against which she was struggling. It was her right to choose. She did become involved with the male who worked at the health club where she was employed. After several dates, they had a sexual encounter. Her first with a male. She did not reach orgasm and reported anxiety with penetration. She felt like she was losing control of her own body. With repeated encounters she relaxed and enjoyed intercourse, realizing that the surrender she felt need not define her total relationship. She had no desire to cut off her contacts with her lesbian friends. They furnished her with a different kind of emotional support than she obtained from Cliff, her new male friend. She told Cliff about her therapy and he volunteered to come in for several sessions.

Cliff was tall, but a little shorter than Pearl. He said this had bothered him at first, but not anymore: "I never intended to date her when we first met. We were just friends. She's really easy to talk to and we have so much in common. After being with Pearl at work, I felt bored going out with other girls. Now most women look so small to me. Most women can't hold a candle to her. She's beautiful."

Pearl's self-esteem increased immeasurably once she learned she could function normally in a relationship with a man. She had reacted to the initial rejection from males by doubting and rejecting herself, almost to the point of giving up. Her experience with Cliff, however, was highly romanticized. He was her Prince Charming who had rescued her from an unhappy life. She was now genuinely happy. Pearl is an example of how achieving a stereotype and fulfilling the cultural ideal can yield happiness and contentment. Perhaps being denied access to the role made it seem all the more desirable.

Our ability to assume gender-based roles successfully is dependent upon our awareness of the roles in which we have previously functioned. Without this awareness, we carry over behaviors and expectations from one role to another. This occurs whether or not the roles are gender based. Gender identity is formed in childhood and reinforced through all subsequent developmental stages. Our expectations of self and others are continually tainted with obsolete or inappropriate gender-specific behaviors. This is borne out by the corporate jokes about female vice presidents who are still expected to make coffee or provide a good time for male colleagues.   These inappropriate gender based beliefs and expectations create a hostile environment for women in the workplace.

Mary worked in a law firm in which she was consistently reminded of her gender even though it had no bearing on her work performance. Her male colleagues consistently told her how sexy she looked or how distracting it was for them to try to work with her around. Since she was fresh from law school and had taken a course, "Women in Law," which graphically outlined the problems women lawyers face in a male-dominated profession, she acted immediately. She had her secretary type up a memo based on the U.S. Equal Employment Opportunities Commissions (EEOC) on Title VII of the Civil Rights Amendment. She sent a copy to each member of her firm, clarifying that she would not hesitate to file a complaint with EEOC if their unwanted sexual attentions continued. She warned them. It was very effective. For the most part, her male colleagues respected her assertiveness, and the managing partner was quick to reinforce her position. Mary was fearful of retaliation, particularly that she would be barred from eventual partnership in the firm because she refused to accept gender based discrimination. But she knew she could not work in an environment that consistently focused on her gender rather than her professional competence. It took courage for her to step out of female role behavior and assert her rights.

Unfortunately, most women do not have Mary's awareness. Women are conditioned to accept unwanted male advances. Gender conditioning is so pervasive that most people do not recognize when it is affecting their behavior. Gender contamination in the work setting occurs consistently, but it is only one of many factors that create role strain and prevent comfortable role fit.

Business relationships are difficult to classify. Are they consensual or nonconsensual? There is certainly a consensual element at the outset. We go through a screening process to hire an employee, just as that employee goes through a selection process in finding an employer. Beyond that point, however, the work relationship becomes nonconsensual. We are assigned to supervisors selected by corporation, company, or agency directors. Likewise, supervisors rarely have the option of selecting employees assigned to their division. This is true whether we work in a public or private sector, in academia, or in business. Our business relationship counterparts are not of our own choosing. They quickly lose the consensual element present in the initial stage of relationship formation.

Moreover, once we become involved in the process of working with a specific relationship counterpart, we cannot easily terminate that relationship. There would be considerable risk and consequence to our immediate livelihood, as well as to our record of employment, which trails behind us on our career path. Disturbances in business relationships, whether they result in failure or not, impact seriously on self-esteem and productivity.

Let's look at a disturbance in a business relationship and clarify the level of delusionary thinking that promoted the disturbance.

Joanne was a nurse consultant who worked for a large pharmaceutical company. Her job description included sales and promotion as well as customer service. She was best at customer service and did an outstanding job in pleasing her accounts. She spent a great deal of time getting to know the people she interacted with in the agencies she serviced. However, whenever it came time to introduce a new product or inform her accounts of cost increases, she engaged in avoidance and denial, so much so that she appeared at times to be more identified with the interests of her accounts than the interests of the company that paid her salary. On one such occasion, she was confronted by her supervisor and required to seek outside counseling to improve her attitude. She was extremely resentful, "I don't need this job. We can get along fine on my husband's salary. My supervisor can't get along with anybody. She has unrealistic expectations of herself and others. The company is already making enough money; we don't have to increase costs to these accounts. And I don't like pressuring our clients to buy new products."

As I listened, it became clear that Joanne had deluded herself into thinking she could and should make policy decisions rather than carry out the directives handed down to her through her supervisor. How did she come to have these unrealistic expectations? Her job description clearly set out her duties and responsibilities. Generally speaking, she had good sense and reality orientation. But she had an overblown sense of entitlement which came from being a homemaker, wife, and mother. Although she did not earn the major portion of the family's income, she had more than fifty percent of the say in the expenditure of disposable income. Neither her husband nor her children objected to her control over the finances, so she had grown accustomed to both policy making and expenditure decisions in her private life. The few clashes that there had been in the family setting were resolved by her withholding affection and sexual favors in the case of her husband. She had overgeneralized this mode of operation and carried it into the workplace, withdrawing and threatening to quit whenever there was a difficult situation and her services were really needed. This occurred when she was expected to perform that portion of her job that she disliked. This time she had gone too far. Her new supervisor had no history with her or any reason to expend time and energy trying to cajole Joanne into more reasonable behavior. She just wanted the job done, so she placed Joanne on probation after giving her an unsatisfactory performance evaluation.

I was surprised that Joanne did not simply quit as she had threatened to do so many times. When I asked her about it, she said she felt like a failure and did not understand what had gone wrong: "I really did a good job and everyone liked me. When I was hired I was told that I would be in complete charge of all my accounts and that they wanted somebody who was capable of independent thought. And when I try to think for myself, I get placed on probation. How unfair. How totally unfair."

I asked Joanne if she had fulfilled her job description. She flushed and acknowledged that she had failed to do so in certain areas which she resented. She described a process wherein she had screened out feedback from her business environment that focused specifically on the areas she disliked. On occasion, she would do just enough to get by. So effective was her denial system that she was amazed and horrified when she received a poor performance review. She preferred to believe that the problem resided with her supervisor, whom she characterized as unfair and unreasonable. Supervisors were supposed to bring out the best in their supervisee, not to be critical and confrontive. As we talked, Joanne gradually began to see her position more clearly. She had not fulfilled her job description because she had never accepted it. She had been immature and uncooperative in pressured situations when the rest of the staff was working to meet a deadline. Her expectations that she could do only those parts of her job that she liked the most and manipulate her way out of the responsibilities she disliked were delusional.

But there was also something wrong with the system in which Joanne worked, because her delusions had not been adequately confronted at the outset of her employment with the company. Her first supervisor, the woman who had hired her, had tried ineffectively to confront her but was defeated by Joanne's manipulations. After each deadline was met, a sense of relief and camaraderie prevailed and the incidents seemed to be forgotten. Joanne was hard to confront. She either cried or threatened to leave. On occasion she would apologize and promise to do better. Ineffective supervision was a major component in this business relationship disturbance. Joanne's unrealistic expectations, along with her denial system, were confronted in counseling. She did not quit her job, nor was she fired. Instead, she went on to reach a greater level of competence under a more effective supervisor who confronted her weaknesses as well as reinforced her strengths.

Joanne's experience in the role of wife, mother, and homemaker had conditioned her to see herself as more autonomous than she could be in a paid work setting. At home she worked at her own pace and on her own schedule. She made major financial decisions and directed the at-home behavior of her husband and children. When she joined the staff of a pharmaceutical company she experienced role strain. She was expected to carry out policies set by others and had no input in decisions that affected her interactions with her accounts. She experienced role shock when she was assigned to a new supervisor who was unwilling to accept partial performance. Her poor performance review and subsequent probationary status, along with counseling that was both supportive and confrontive enabled her to establish realistic expectations in her job as a nurse consultant. As she consolidated her new identity, her relationship with her supervisor improved, at first gradually and then exponentially. What aided Joanne in her transition from delusionary thinking to a realistic orientation to her business environment? How did she finally achieve role fit? Confronting the truth about her inappropriate expectations allowed her to make an adjustment. It is regrettable that, like many others, Joanne suffered so much discomfort in the process before effective confrontation occurred.

Where does the responsibility rest for assessment and reeducation of individuals like Joanne? With herself, the business community, or our educational system? *What do you think?* Delusional expectations occur in the work setting as readily as they do in family and personal relationships. Gender-based stereotypes and romantic symbols create situations in which fantasy and automatic role behavior diminish productivity at work and damage ongoing personal relationships at home. The office romance furnishes a clear example of delusional relating.

Let's look at Roger and Lila. Roger was a very sensitive male who did not, on the surface, fit the masculine stereotype. When he was younger, in college, he used to enjoy poetry and had little interest in sports. After graduation he took a job as personnel manager with a sporting goods company. Because of his calm, quiet demeanor, he was very successful in working with people. His ability to be both supportive and encouraging was recognized by his supervisors. After several years he was promoted to an administrative position where most of his contact was with administrative peers rather than with people he counseled. Moreover, most of his peers were men who were more bound than he by restrictions of the male stereotype. They all had a strong interest in sports and had gravitated toward the company because of its locker room atmosphere and sports-oriented ambiance. For Roger, the emphasis on athletics had been less an attraction than a drawback.

Increased money and prestige came with Roger's new position, and at first he really enjoyed those benefits. Then he began to experience role strain. His job was to facilitate communication and motivate his peers to greater levels of productivity. In his prior position as personnel director, he had had more contact with middle management, many of whom were made up of women. Roger felt more comfortable around women because they seemed less competitive. He could fall back on male role behavior, engaging in light flirtatious exchanges where he sympathized with the problems they were having at work or with the men in their lives. It was a role in which he felt comfortable.

Roger felt less adequate in his new role. The only woman he saw regularly was Lila, his administrative assistant. She was young, competent and very restricted by female role behavior. Roger liked that. She deferred to him, not just because he was her boss, but because he was a man. This was just what Roger needed: someone to make him feel more like a man at a time when he was doubting himself.

They didn't sexualize the relationship fully, but over time, they diverted more and more energy into their relationship with each other and less into meeting their job requirements or developing themselves professionally. This went on for years. There were other changes. As their conversations became more personal they felt less need to communicate with their respective spouses and their marriage relationships suffered. Roger also changed in other ways. Because he felt inadequate around his sports oriented male peers, he began to listen to games on the radio, watch them on television, and avidly read the sports page: all things he had not done as a younger man. He no longer read poetry. He was relying on the male stereotype because he did not know what else to do. His dress and demeanor became more like "one of the boys." He became less effective at communicating and his people skills diminished. What had happened?

Roger's business role had changed, and it was a poor fit. He felt he had to change his personality to do his new job. How ironic: he had been selected for the job because he was different-a sensitive male who could communicate. His supervisors had hoped he would teach the men in upper management to communicate more effectively. Instead, he had lost his sensitivity and abandoned his core identity. He lost more than that: one Friday he went home and found a note from his wife. She had left for a few days to visit friends and hoped he would be gone when she returned. She wanted a divorce. He was no longer the man she had married. She found him boring. She had spent one too many baseball seasons without contact or companionship. She wanted to get out of the relationship before it was too late. She feared she would also change as he had. She loved him, but it was over. Roger was in shock.

His life had changed radically. It had started slowly, with role strain. Had Roger focused on the problem, he might have resolved it or achieved a better role fit at work. Instead, he distracted himself from the real issue by becoming involved with Lila in an office romance. His subsequent efforts to fit in with "the boys" and abandon his own personality compounded the problem. His marriage ended because he stopped sharing his feelings with his wife and put little or no energy into being her friend and companion. Roger developed severe role shock, but his reaction to promotion and role change is not unusual. Promoting from within does not always work. A large percentage of people who are advanced to upper-management positions are not suited for them, nor are they prepared for the changes they will experience in their new jobs. An assumption is made that they will adjust and produce as they did in their prior positions, but it is not easy to move a person from one role to another. Role shock is a common occurrence.

What about Lila? She also suffered because of Roger's poor adjustment to his new job. She became his distraction, and as a result, she failed to develop her skills as an administrative assistant and wasted several years of her career development in mindless female role behavior. Her relationship with Roger ended with his resignation and divorce. She was reassigned to another division of the company. Her own marriage had been severely weakened by long periods of neglect during which she fantasized about having an ongoing relationship with Roger. She had compared her own husband unfavorably with her boss because she saw him as less successful. Her marriage continued, but it took several years to reestablish it as a viable relationship. She had lost precious time in career development and had deeply hurt her husband, Harry, who, like Roger's wife, felt the loss of companionship and intimacy. Lila had deluded herself into thinking that her boss, Roger, was something he was not; romantic, secure, understanding, and caring. All these were qualities she had felt were missing in her own husband. In reality, Roger was insecure and self absorbed. Had Lila seen Roger clearly or evaluated the circumstances of their clandestine office romance, she would have realized that they were both acting without integrity, both personally or professionally. Lila did not, however, step out of the female role long enough to realize what she was doing. It was not until years later that she understood the meaning of her behavior: "I had reached a point in my marriage where the magic was gone. Harry and I cared about each other, but his hair was getting thin and I was putting on a few pounds. I needed reassurance that I was still attractive as a woman. I also felt trapped in my job. Administrative assistants are glorified secretaries. I wasn't going anywhere unless I got more education. But I hated the thought of going back to school or even looking for another job. I had nothing much to put on my resume. All I could hope for was a lateral move. So instead of dealing with my issues, I involved myself with Roger. I fooled myself into thinking he would rescue me. How could I have been so stupid?" Her voice broke and she started to cry. The mascara ran down her face and she looked quite forlorn. I was aware of a deep sadness. I have worked with many women who, like Lila, who mindlessly engaged in female role behavior, over and over again, in hopes of receiving a reward by pleasing a male, rather than developing themselves. Lila had wasted so much time. It would not, however, have been helpful for her to focus on blaming herself; she needed to use her insight in a positive way. Not wanting to cut off her feeling, I remained silent. She continued crying. Several minutes later, she said: "They didn't fire me--but I really wasn't doing my job. I could see what was happening to Roger, how he was getting off-track and pretending to be something he wasn't, a dumb, macho pig. But instead of confronting him, I played cutesy games and tried to be his mother and his girlfriend. If I'd had my head on straight, we'd both have better jobs today."

Lila was probably right, but people in delusional relationships do not have their "heads on straight." They are living in fantasy and acting out stereotypes. Normal problem solving abilities are in suspension.

Perhaps you should examine your own business relationships for similar problems. How would you assess the role fit you currently have in your job?

What constitutes good employment role fit: knowing what your strengths are and determining if your job description utilizes them. Realizing your weaknesses and determining if your current job requires strengths and abilities that you do not have and cannot develop. Just because you are a productive and successful member of a team does not mean that someday, if you work hard, you can lead that team. Many employees expect to learn the ropes and advance to supervisory or vice presidential level. They may even see themselves as chief executive officers. However, it takes a certain cluster of characteristics to fill most job descriptions comfortably. Moving individuals from one level to another with minimal on-the-job training creates situations like the one in which Roger found himself. Who was responsible for the bad fit? Did the company have a responsibility to Roger and Lila to protect them from their own role dependency, or does responsibility lie with the individual employee? Does our educational system have a responsibility to prepare us more adequately for role change, which is a natural occurrence throughout our lives.

We have explored two cases of on-the-job role strain that progressed to role shock. Joanne, the nurse consultant, was able to resolve her difficulty and achieve satisfactory role fit. Aided by a supportive supervisor and outside counseling, she gained insight into her delusionary expectations and went on to a more productive work experience. Roger's case was more complex. There were several layers of delusionary thinking that contributed to his demise. Unintentionally, he presented himself in a non-genuine manner, based on his version of the male stereotype; quiet, calm, cool, supportive, always agreeable and encouraging others. It was a style he had cultivated to conceal his lack of confidence and low self-esteem, it worked quite well. In his role as personnel director, he could maintain the facade and rely on the counselor role to fulfill his duties. He had a good relationship with his wife. Their shared interests in literature and art provided a stable basis to their marriage. After the promotion, he felt uprooted and tried to compensate by assuming still another role, one of the sports-oriented guys. It felt foreign to him and he was unable to adjust. He could not fulfill his primary job objective, of modeling and facilitating communication skills for his peers, because he had lost sight of that part of himself. Rather than focus on the issue or seek help from his supervisor, he distracted himself with an office romance, falling back on still another male role prescription, man on the make. These fragments of role behavior were insufficient to support Roger in times of stress. What he needed was a clear sense of his own identity and an understanding of the impact his new job was having on him. Without that self-knowledge and understanding, he was unable to function, professionally or personally.

It is unclear whether Roger would have made a better adjustment if he had received appropriate preparation for the transition. His supervisors made assumptions about his ability to produce at a comparable level in a very different environment. Their expectations proved unrealistic. Roger's self-esteem, which was already low, suffered irreparable damage as a result of his inability to perform adequately in his new job. It would seem that both Roger and his supervisors would have benefitted from exposure to the basic principles of role expectation and role fit. Unfortunately, these concepts are not fully understood or integrated in any aspect of our culture. Our personal, as well as professional, adjustment would be greatly enhanced and much human suffering would be avoided if our educational system provided an adequate knowledge base for daily living. The principles of role taking and gender expectations are certainly as important as multiplication tables and the ABCs.

Chapter 3

Shaping Gender Identity

You have suddenly discovered that the world is divided into two kinds of people, men and women. This division is made on the basis of their genitals. There are other visible indicators of the difference, like hairstyle and clothing, but as far as you can tell there seem to be more similarities than differences. You can't figure out what the big fuss is all about, but you do know that you have to be like everybody else. This means you will have to keep many of your thoughts and feelings a secret because they don't fit with what is expected of you by the folks that matter. You hope you don't forget about the hidden parts of yourself: you want to remember what you are really like. Sometimes, you might just want to be yourself.

Gender-specific expectations are fostered in countless ways by our educational system. As children, we strain to meet the expectations of those around us.

Let me tell you about Jeff and how he experienced role strain. Notice how seriously it affected him. He was trying to learn how to be a man. The athletic stereotype was his goal. This is what he said: "If you aren't good at sports and you don't have the right clothes, they treat you like dirt." It was hard to be a boy and do it right. You had to practice sports a lot and be really good so the kids will respect you, and then you have to convince your folks to buy you the right stuff or you're a wannabe." The serious, unsmiling face and clear blue eyes of thirteen-year-old Jeff communicated the pressure he felt to be popular in his sixth grade class.

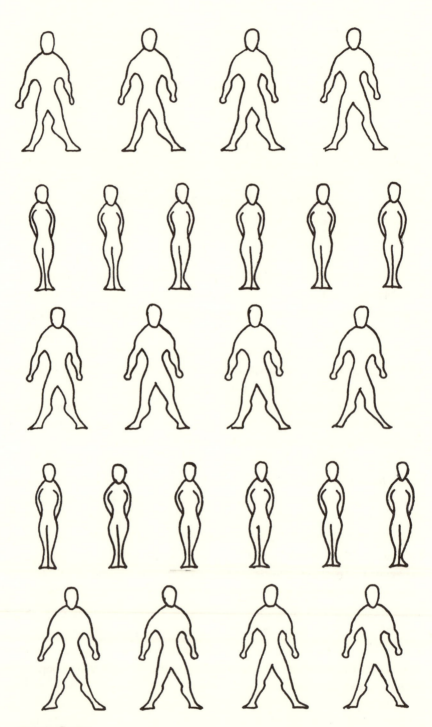

Cookie Cutter

Jeff had a lot of problems figuring out how to do it right. He was very good at basketball. In fact, it surprised him to discover how well he played and what a difference it made in how he was treated by his classmates, the teachers, and even the principal, when he made points or blocked skillfully. He liked to hear his name shouted out when he was about to score or block an opponent's shot. For him, recognition and praise were becoming drug like and he was as driven to obtain the high as a cocaine addict.

Jeff was big for his age. His well developed arms, legs, and chest muscles had been trained in karate, a common activity for young boys in our culture. He had to work hard to control spontaneous karate responses while playing basketball or other sports. Repeated fouls were spoiling his game. Although he understood about fair play and sportsmanship, aggressive impulses surfaced and he roughly shoved a member of the opposing team. This is how he explained it: "He fouled me, but nobody saw it. He was after me, not just the way you go after someone in ordinary play. He wanted my ass." It was startling to see and hear this young boy transformed into a caricature of the male stereotype. He was confused. Jeff had followed the rules and tried to do it right but now the drive to succeed, as he understood it, had taken over and his previous child identity was submerged. In its place there was a conflicted, disjointed, and very unhappy young man. His aggressive behavior was jeopardizing his position on the team. "If they won't let me play, I can't go back. Those guys will beat me up. I'd be a piece of shit. I'm not going back." His voice rasped, his eyes teared, he held his face in his hands. He was truly desperate.

Life and identity depended on being a successful athlete. How had Jeff come to believe this was the only way to be male? Most of his toys had been gender specific or sports oriented ever since he was a toddler. He had been given one piece of sports equipment after another. The only time his father spent with him related to sports. His father and grandfather went to games of all sorts and knew the popular sports heroes.

Everyone in the community seemed to revere guys who did well for the home team. And the first and strongest thrill of pride came when Jeff scored for the school basketball team. Movies, television, everything gave out the message that the best males were sports oriented. Starting with Little League on up, ball games were serious business. Better be good at it or you won't be taken seriously. In fact, you would be ridiculed, pitied, and discarded. That's what happened to girls and women, even moms.

That was another really confusing message that Jeff received from all sides in different forms. Moms had to be obeyed, and yet they were not really important.

Dads were better than moms. Girls weren't anything yet. They would grow up to be fucked and become moms. But Jeff really loved his mom, more than he did his Dad, because she was nicer and was always there. It made Jeff mad that he was expected to do so many opposing things simultaneously. How could he love and respect his mother and yet hold her in contempt at the same time? The confusion quickly turned to anger. He had also been given messages to control his anger and be decisive at the same time. Sometimes, the conflict became so intense that he acted on impulse just to resolve the pressure he felt. Like the time he was in class and the teacher sent him to the principal's office for misbehavior. One of his classmates had grabbed his book and created a disturbance. The teacher didn't believe him. It was unfair. Jeff honestly thought he was in the right and that he was being treated with disrespect.

He was conflicted. He had repeatedly been told by his athletic coaches and cub scout master to think for himself, and defend his honor, so he did. Jeff left the school instead of going to the principal's office. He went home. It seemed like a good choice to him. He could not allow the teacher and the principal to shame him. That wouldn't be manly. It was against the rules, but no one understood. Everyone was mad at him. His parents said they were disappointed. And, of course, there were consequences. He had to understand that good kids didn't just walk out of school. They respected teachers. He didn't get that rifle he had been promised for the next hunting season. Jeff did not respect the teacher. He hated her. Wanted to kill her. Of course he wouldn't do that. He wasn't that impulsive, but he was very angry and confused about how to express his feelings.

His parents were well meaning and totally unaware of the damage that stereotyping and myth perpetuation was causing their son. They had expected Jeff to be more balanced. He had good sense--why didn't he use it? They had furnished him with every opportunity to learn how to be a good boy: church, school, cub scouts, little league, karate. Why was he so angry and oppositional? How could they correct it--or was it too late? What was going on inside Jeff?

Jeff no longer trusted his parents to make good choices for him. Nor did he trust the school or his coaches to treat him fairly. No matter what anyone said, or did not say, Jeff knew that ultimately he was on his own. He alone would have to sort through the conflicting sets of directions and rules about how to make it in the world--and he could not count on anyone to understand if he made a mistake. No one would cut him any slack. He was disappointed and hurt, but the worst feeling of all was shame. Shame that he couldn't do it right--couldn't be successful at being male. He cried silently, hot salty tears, and then he stopped himself. He didn't want anyone to know how much it mattered. Men were not supposed to care.

We usually do not think of children and adolescents suffering from role strain, but when the expectations of the role taker, regardless of age, are exaggerated, unrealistic, or based in stereotype or fantasy, crisis does occur. Very often the role bearer is unaware that the expectations are unrealistic and perceives the disturbance or failure as a sign of personal inadequacy. This is a very important point. Role takers usually blame themselves, not the stereotype, for their failure. Unfortunately, relationship counterparts, parents, children, siblings, or spouses frequently continue to apply pressure to the role bearer in an attempt to force conformity to the stereotype. Often this pressure is applied without awareness.

Sometimes this results in compliance, at great personal cost to the role bearer, permanent damage to self-esteem, and even suicide. Role strain casualties are often self-inflicted. It is not uncommon for role bearers to apply extreme pressure to themselves in a desperate attempt to fulfill a stereotype. Marilyn Monroe is a case in point. She was both the archetype and the satirist of emphasized femininity. She played and lived one version of the female role, the sex symbol version. Finally, she was no longer able to fulfill the role because of fatigue, aging, and the psychological strain of suppressing all other aspects of her identity to this one part--exaggerated femininity. She chose suicide as a better option than continuing to live the stereotype.

There are many less sensational cases of role strain and role shock that have occurred in communities both throughout the United States and abroad.

The incidence of role strain increases when adolescence is reached. Our hormone levels shift. We are beset with increased cultural pressure to grow up and take on gender-based role behaviors. More cross-gender contact is expected of us, and at the same time we must separate from our parents and become more autonomous. We do not accept parental guidance very readily at this age because our developmental task is to form our own identities. We are, therefore, without adequate support at a significant cultural juncture. Molly is a case in point.

Molly was sixteen when she first attempted suicide. After an argument with her boyfriend, who had angrily accused her of coming on to another boy, she went home and took a bottle of her mother's prescription medicine, slit her wrists in several places, and crawled into bed. This was not a cry for help: she really wanted to die. Her older sister came home early from a date and discovered Molly. She thought it unusual that her sister had gone to bed so early, sensed something strange, moved closer, and noticed the blood stains. She called an ambulance and Molly was rushed to the emergency room.

A few days later, when I met with the family in my office, we tried to clarify why Molly wanted to die. She was doing well in school as far as grades and social contacts were concerned. There were no major problems in the family. Both parents were caring and involved. Molly got along well with her sister. But there had been signs that Molly was upset and depressed about the relationship with her seventeen-year-old boyfriend, Pete. They had been dating for over a year and had many fights, some of which had escalated to the point of violence. They seemed oblivious to the consequences. They fought even while driving the car which, on more than one occasion, led to an accident. Pete was possessive and jealous. If Molly did not behave the way he thought she should, he would yell at her, push or even slap her. These are stereotypic behaviors.

Molly, in turn would cry and eventually came to believe it was all her fault. Those arguments usually ended with Molly trying to comfort her boyfriend and help him figure out why he had lost control. His behavior was that of a two-year-old having a temper tantrum. Her behavior, like that of a hysterical wife-mother figure, was protective and indirectly controlling.

I was struck with how stereotypically gender based their reactions were. Pete was exhibiting his brand of high school macho, based on his understanding of what he was supposed to do as a male. By exaggerating a male response to stay in control and dominate women, he was desperately trying to meet the cultural prescription for male role behavior. But he was coming across more like an obstinate child. This was a time in his life when parents, teachers, peers, everyone around him was putting increased pressure on him to grow up and be a man. Molly was also feeling intense pressure to be a woman, which, as far as she could tell, meant standing by her man, understanding him, and taking care of him even when this seemed to violate and restrict her rights as a person. She felt that she was failing miserably at growing up and wanted to die rather than accept failure at what she perceived to be her most important role in life.

Molly's parents wanted her to end the relationship, but Molly felt bonded to Pete. He would not leave her alone even after both sets of parents and the school counselor had intervened. The combined pressure exceeded Molly's ability to cope. Death seemed like her only choice.

She said, "I'm the daughter from hell. My parents try so hard, but I just can't be what they want. I've tried to break it off, but something inside makes me take him back. I'm all he has, but I just can't make him happy. The things he wants from me don't seem right. He says I'm not understanding enough. What am I supposed to do? It seems so unfair. I'm a person, too, aren't I?"

The more Molly talked about her feelings, the clearer it became that she was suffering from role strain. Her depression began when she realized that she had to subvert her natural strengths and abilities in order not to threaten her boyfriend. She tried to go along with his lead, but since she was as bright, if not more so, than he was, it was hard for her to take the role and play the games. Her conflict erupted in arguments and temper tantrums similar to those she had when she was two-years-old.

Molly and Pete were both responding to cultural injunctions and attempting to force themselves into stereotypic behaviors. They had been attracted to one another because each superficially appeared to approximate an ideal image. Actually, they were interchangeable with Popeye and Olive Oyle, Tarzan and Jane, Donald and Daisy Duck, or any of the extreme, often ludicrous, model sets our culture offers to pattern ourselves after. Neither party knew much about the other and most of their interactions had been governed by role taking. Their relationship ended, of course, before they ever knew each other as real people. Without insight or intervention, this pattern could go on indefinitely. One delusional relationship after another.

Any reaction? Think about your own awareness of role pressure and role strain when you were that age. Are you still trying to fulfill the same cultural stereotype?

In looking at these studies of role strain, we can isolate several factors that are useful in assessing our own relationships. The extent to which we are bound by, or hold others to, gender-restrictive stereotypes is limited by the extent of awareness we have of that process in ourselves. Much of the process is preconscious: we must focus in order to detect it. Self-awareness is a necessary component in treating delusionary relationships.

Our educational system does not value self-knowledge. Our awareness level of the thoughts and feelings that guide our behavior is quite low. In fact, we all respond to preconscious programming without recognizing what we are doing.

Women are programmed to believe that they need a man to survive. This is based on the assumption that women cannot provide for themselves or protect themselves from male predators who will either rape, enslave, or kill them. This may have been true when women were chattels and had no legal rights. Womens' position has changed, but the preconscious belief systems have not. Cultural programming imparts the urgent message that as soon as a female reaches pubescence and can reproduce, her main purpose in life is to attract and keep a male to protect and provide for her. Similarly, men are programmed to be providers and protectors regardless of their physical size, strength, or inclination. These overgeneralized messages are transmitted to all males and females indiscriminately. Rather primitive educational system, wouldn't you say?

Although the transmission process varies, the message, woman needs man; man must have his mate, is universal. It forms the basis for delusionary needs and fantasies.

Let's look at Amelia's fantasy and how she passed it on to her daughter. In order to understand Amelia, try to identify with her and her life experience. Amelia knew she lived in fantasy. She both laughed and cried about it in our sessions. "I know it's not going anywhere," she said of one of her many relationships with truck drivers who frequented the motel in which she worked as a housekeeper. However, they gave her the feeling of being young, attractive, and desirable. That was very important to her. It was how she measured her self esteem.

"The fools, they are in love with me," she said as she gloried in the fact that they wanted her sexually. She seemed oblivious to their exploitation of her. Amelia accepted money and favors from them. Although she needed that to supplement her income, it was not the reason she did it. "It gives me power," she said, "I have something they want, and they will do anything for it. I know I can please them."

Being a sex object started when she was a little girl. Her father and older brothers had used her sexually and rewarded her with attention, trinkets, and candy. It was amazing how much her adult sexual behavior paralleled what had happened to her as a child. As a Hispanic, she had been consistently taught to subordinate her own needs to those of the males in her family. To anticipate what they wanted and try to please them. She did not understand why her mother, an Anglo, did not do the same thing or passively obey to avoid beatings and poor treatment. Instead, Amelia's mother ran away when she was eleven and was not heard from again.

Amelia never identified with her mother. Her own skin was dark like her father's, and she tried very hard to learn Spanish at school and at home because her father preferred it. She finished high school with top grades in honors courses. This seemed significant to me because her father never supported her academic excellence and failed to attend a single school program, including her graduation. Her mind was not a consideration to him. It was only her body that interested him, both sexually and for the house work and yard work she could do. Amelia did not go on to college, although she had scholarship opportunities and was clearly capable of succeeding academically. Instead, she cleaned house for her father and eventually married one of his friends, a man nineteen years her senior. She was fulfilling the role expectations that her father had for her, rather than following her natural inclinations and abilities.

What happened to Amelia? Did she succumb to the cultural pressures and dutifully resign herself to a life of sexual servitude and menial support to a father surrogate, or did she resist and attempt to develop a life of her own? Although she tried, Amelia found she could not be content as a wife and mother. It never occurred to her to openly resist. That went against the passivity and acceptance she had learned. Instead, She began to be self destructive. She drank, at first just a little, but enough to get her through the rough times.

As time went on, she developed the habit of literally disappearing for several days at a time. She told me in session that she would enter a bar, catch someone's eye, and seduce him. She liked younger men to compensate for the fact that her earlier sexual encounters had been limited to older men. In return she would receive money and attention. It was a much better life than being married, where she received little positive attention and no money. Divorce was not an option because she was Catholic, and besides, she could not afford the legal procedure. But she did end her marriage by simply leaving and not going back. For a while she lived in a shelter for abused women, where she was exposed to feminist doctrine and slowly began to realize how she had been abused and exploited. It made her angry. She was angry with men but continued to use the feminine role and exaggerated femininity to attract and seduce them.

She did not see herself as a prostitute, since she worked regularly cleaning houses and motels to support herself. The money she received from the men she sexualized with furnished extras for herself and her children, whom she called and saw intermittently. Amelia did not totally forsake the mother role or the behaviors that went with it. She still loved her children, gave them advice, and shared the money she earned with them. She did not, however, live with them, nor did she build her life around them.

It was through one of her children, a daughter, that I first began my work with the family. Rosa, seventeen, and herself an honor student, had inherited much of her mother's confusion about female role behavior. Like her mother, she was particularly unclear about what males could actually contribute to her sense of well-being. She was dark and attractive like her mother and usually had a boyfriend, generally one who was younger than she and made poor grades in school. Her current boyfriend was less bright, less articulate, and essentially less adaptive and competent than Rosa. He seemed superfluous to her life. "You have to have a guy around," she said, "or the other girls don't respect you." Sexually, she enjoyed masturbating more than partner sex. It was more intense and less messy; moreover, she didn't have to worry about pregnancy or sexually transmitted disease.

Like her mother, Amelia, Rosa was well on her way to becoming totally self-sufficient, but she was not at peace with this. She felt something was missing. She wasn't quite complete. The cultural pronouncement that a woman needs a man and cannot really function without a protector and provider had resulted in a restless unmet need in both Rosa and her mother. This need was not grounded in reality.

Had the culture created an artificial need in Amelia and Rosa? Both women seemed to have the idea that they were incomplete without male attendance in their lives. The males to whom they did relate to were abusive and exploitative, significantly different from the historic provider and protector ideal. That ideal was outdated, but it was still at work. The overgeneralized message that women are non functional without fathers, husbands, or some other form of cookie cutter male affected Amelia and Rosa as it affects all other women. They mindlessly sought a token male, whose presence failed to enhance their lives. Instead, their male cohorts hindered their self-development and distracted them from a sense of peace and contentment.

Women like Amelia and Rosa have little opportunity to know or value men as individuals. Instead, men become romantic symbols and are valued for their roles as protectors and providers, whether or not they actually function as such.

When people talk about their gender identity and try to recall the origin of their basic ideas about being male or female, they think about their parents. Comparisons are made, and negative and positive similarities are drawn. It is an extremely illuminating process, often accompanied by emotional upheaval. Intense feelings are associated with childhood memories. Identity formation is shaped by emotionally charged experiences. Gender-specific shaping is particularly emotional. This is due to the sex-negative bias of our culture, in which everything about sex carries an extra emotional charge. Messages about gender identity encoded in our childhood experiences endure throughout our subsequent development.

At twenty-six, Bob was beginning to feel like an old man. He felt as if he had not accomplished very much for his age. He had an undergraduate degree in business, a low-paying job, and no girlfriend. He had expected to be married by now, but his girlfriend, Audrey, had ended their relationship and announced plans to go back to school and get a master's degree. She was also moving back in with her parents to help finance her graduate training. Audrey and Bob had shared a town house. Bob could not afford to live there without sharing expenses with someone. He did not want a new roommate, nor did he want to downscale his standard of living. He felt like quitting his job and moving out of town. "Not that I have any place to go," he said, "or anyone to go with." He sat in my office, looking dejected.

I asked him what he expected of himself. He was silent for a while, a long while. When he began to speak, he sounded angry and impatient with himself. "At my age, my father had two kids. He knew where he was going in life. He didn't make a lot of money, but he fed us and Mom didn't have to work. I can't even support myself." He covered his face with his hands. He was feeling shame. I said nothing.   After a while, he spoke again: "My Mom would never have left my Dad. They had a lot going for each other."

I reflected the process I was witnessing back to him. "You're comparing yourself to your father, and you don't like the way you are stacking up." He looked at me and nodded. Bob felt very inadequate compared to his father. His father's ability to keep a woman, sire, and support children, went far beyond what Bob had accomplished. There were, of course, other men Bob's age who would have felt accomplished if they had graduated from college and procured Bob's job. It was all relative. Bob's standard was his father, and he did not measure up. Consequently, he felt he was less of a man. He seemed lost in reminiscences of the past and he wanted to talk about his father. Perhaps he was looking for answers or maybe he did not want to deal with the painful present. I just listened.

He remembered a time when he was ten. The whole family was at the state fair and some big biker types had pushed his six-year-old sister out of a ticket line. She started to cry. There were three bikers and Bob's father was alone. He approached the men, laying his arm on his daughter's shoulder, he said to one of them, "Now you don't want to make a little girl cry, do you?" Bob remembered how the bikers had looked at his father. They seemed surprised. Bob was scared. He thought there would be a fight. His father just stood there looking at the men for what seemed like an eternity. Finally, one of the bikers said, "Sorry, Captain, not looking for trouble." His father nodded and got in line in front of the men. Bob felt proud of his father and always saw him as a strong and brave man. A man to be reckoned with. That was the standard to which he held himself. There was no direct connection between that incident and what Bob was experiencing in the present. No doubt there were other incidents Bob could have recalled that would have been more similar, perhaps about his father's job or his relationship with his mother, but since those memories were not as highly charged with emotion, they were not recalled. The memory of this incident returned because of the strong feeling of pride Bob had in his father for standing up to the bikers. It contrasted sharply with the strong feeling of shame Bob was currently experiencing because his girlfriend, Audrey, had left him and, as a result, his standard of living had been reduced. His identity as a man had diminished.

Bob was having an over-generalized response. This type of response is very common, particularly when one is in emotional distress. Fragments of cognitive and emotional recall are lifted from memory and come together in confused combinations. There is usually a relationship, but it is not always immediately discernible. The connection was clarified when Bob sorted through his feelings and realized how ashamed he felt. He also gained insight regarding his tendency to compare himself unfavorably to his father. Bob had not consciously patterned himself after his father: he just liked and respected him, absorbing his view of what a man should be from observing his father's behaviors. Whenever Bob was in trouble, he searched his store of memories for a way out. What he remembered was usually linked to his father. This became a negative process because Bob usually concluded that his father would not have gotten himself into the troubled state in the first place. This conclusion was usually followed by an unfavorable self-evaluation.

Bob continued to explore his own thought process. He developed more awareness of his feelings and how they affected his behavior. His opinion of himself increased. His process shifted. Instead of consistently comparing himself to his father, he developed the habit of thinking for himself. His judgments were based on himself and his current circumstances rather than overcharged memories from the past. He treasured the memory of his father all the more because he now believed he was like his father. He was his own man.

Chapter 4

Stereotypes and Romantic Symbols

Symbols stand for or suggest something else by reason of association. The invisible can be made visible by means of a sign. The golden band stands for a pledge that cannot be seen. A red rose or heart stands for love. A feeling that cannot be seen, only felt. Symbols, whether they take the form of an object, sound or behavioral act, have the capacity to excite, objectify, or evoke a response. Very often, people become symbols. A mother becomes a symbol of nurturance. A father symbolizes protection or provision. Children represent immortality. Secretaries symbolize help or support. Most of us would deny that we or our relationship counterparts function as symbols. We might even be insulted if it was suggested that our relationships are built on symbolism. We like to think we have more awareness than to ignore the reality of who we are in favor of a symbolic representation of an abstract idea or a token. How impersonal. How objectifying to be seen as a symbol that stands for or suggests something else, other than ourselves. To be a visible sign of something invisible. To know that our capacity to excite, interest, or arouse is mystical, conventional, dependent on association or accidental resemblance. Personalized symbolism can be either positive or negative.

A woman vice president in a large corporation may doubt her own worth, particularly if she is seen by others as having been selected as a token. An adopted child may feel less valued by adoptive parents because birth parents are not available. A black banker living in white suburbia may feel more like a symbol of integration than a business success. These are representative of obvious stereotypic situations that are easily recognizable. More subtle pervasive

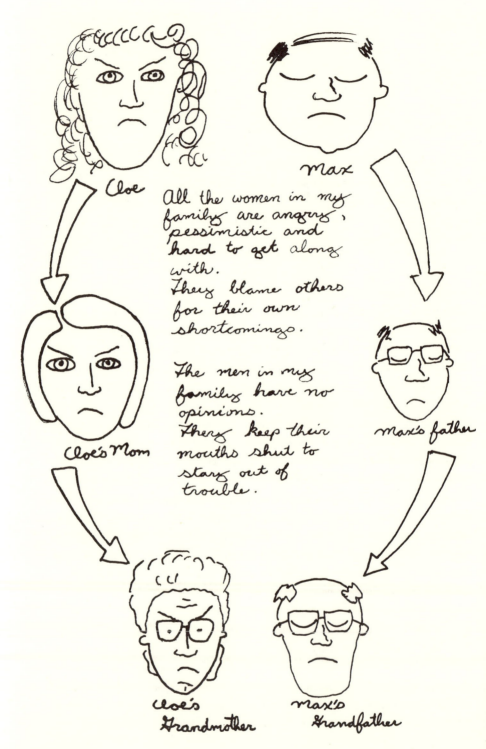

Cloe

Max

All the women in my family are angry, pessimistic and hard to get along with.
They blame others for their own shortcomings.

The men in my family have no opinions.
They keep their mouths shut to stay out of trouble.

Cloe's Mom

Max's father

Cloe's Grandmother

Max's Grandfather

Family Traits

symbolism dominates our conceptualization process regarding all relationships. A love affair is conceptualized as a romantic interlude between two people. Usually there is an association with youth and nonmarital status. Other common associations with affairs are great sex, fun, and light-heartedness.   Less commonly, love affairs are permeated with a sense of purity and high ideals that do not characterize ordinary relationships.   Hence, the strong attraction or longing for romance or an affair when existing relationships become common-place, or when life in general seems dull and uneventful.   People fantasize about relating to someone new or strange and exotic places, mystery and adventure. These romantic concepts have the ability to evoke powerful feelings which, in turn, affect behavior.   Many of these associations are complex.   Unconscious associations have long been utilized by marketing specialists to sell products or services.

When these associations and romantic symbols are attached to a person or relationship, the person is invested with an exalted or metaphysical meaning. The symbolism of the association expresses a general, rather than an actual, truth.   The person around whom this mystical association revolves becomes indistinct and recedes into a complex blend of associations. This is a delusionary process accomplished through the power of romantic symbols and stereotypes.

Separating romantic symbols from reality can destroy a relationship or motivate the participants to search for a sequential symbol to keep their relationship intact.   A torrid love affair can fade and dissipate, or the same two people can make a marriage commitment and invest it with stereotypic sym-bolism, utilizing a home in the suburbs, two children, a van, a dog, and a lawn free of crabgrass.   This state, commitment and marriage, carries its own series of symbolic events and objects that signify success.   The children, the dogs, the lawn, and the house are invested with meaning far beyond their practical or real values.   We become attached to these symbols to the point that they define and delude us.   They also serve as a structure to contain and organize life for those too timid to experience themselves and their relationships realistically.   Too timid to experience specific rather than general truths.

Jason was a hairdresser.   He worked in a family salon owned by his brother and sister-in-law, who were also hairdressers.   Both men and women frequented the shop.   Since Jason specialized in color, he worked on many males whose hair was turning gray.   Jason associated gray hair with wisdom and power.   This is a common association, at least for males.   The associations that Jason had concerning gray hair on women were different.   Gray hair on women signified a loss of power. They were no longer useful as sexual objects if their hair was gray, their primary worth resided in their ability to attract males. Whenever he thought about it, Jason realized that this was simplistic, but he rarely thought about it. He just had the associations.

When Jason's own hair started to turn gray, he found himself in a quandary about what to do about it. Should he streak it more dramatically and take advantage of the maturity and power image, or should he tint it dark, concealing the gray to evoke a more youthful image? He chose in favor of the gray. Besides the power association, it had a softening effect on the lines of his face.

Jason's sister-in-law, Penny, had small breasts. After she and her husband, Clark, began experiencing marital difficulties and separated, she felt insecure about her ability to attract males. If she were to be single again and have to reenter the dating scene, she felt she would be at a disadvantage because her breasts were so small. So she had breast implant surgery. Large breasts attracted men, they made it clear that they were looking at a woman who had the appropriate sexual equipment. Penny did not enjoy sex but felt it was part of the barter system. Part of attracting a male. "I don't want to fuck them," she said, "I just want them to want to fuck me."

Both Penny and Jason were utilizing common symbols to suggest stereotypes. These symbols had the power to attract attention and seduce potential mates into romantic encounter. It is significant to note that no consideration was given to the consequences of the subterfuge. What happens after someone is attracted by the symbol and drawn into a relationship? The symbol stands for an enticing generality. Neither Jason nor Penny actually fulfilled the stereotypic expectation they evoked with the use of the symbols. Jason was not particularly wise and powerful. Penny was not particularly sexual. The two were projecting half-truths and false images.

Is there a moral issue involved? Should our educational system incorporate units of learning that raise the awareness of our young concerning these issues? We would all benefit from a greater awareness of how symbols control our behavior.

Jerome had a romantic idea about education. He believed that if he got a college education, he would be successful. A good grade point average was symbolic of success. Speaking several foreign languages was symbolic of well-traveled gentry. A rather medieval association, but it was strong enough to motivate Jerome to the long hours of study necessary to pass reading exams in both French and German. He also mastered computer language so he would be literate in the modern sense. Computers symbolized modern technology. A trim body symbolized health. Jason ran to stay in shape. He learned to play golf because it was symbolic of recreation for rich, successful men. He wanted a nice beautiful girl, a trophy, to prove he was worthy of such a woman. Jerome also wanted sex with "slutty" girls to prove he was man enough to run with the big dogs, that is the way he conceptualized it. He even wore a redneck-type billed cap as a badge of his manhood. He did this very selectively since it was a lower-class image and he generally aspired to project upper-or middle-class values. However, the billed cap was a youthful, manly symbol, which compensated for its redneck associations.

There were many symbols in Jerome's life. It was unclear how he had come to value them. Some were obviously the product of his parents' life-style and modeling. Still others came from books he had read or television shows he had watched. Some he adopted from peers or community heroes whom he aspired to emulate. Many of the symbols in his life had been absorbed automatically and unconsciously without any awareness on his part. Like his association with beer and manliness and between Coca-Cola and good times. He did not actually know that blondes were more fun, but he did know that they turned more heads. Well over half the cheerleaders he had seen were blondes. He was really surprised when he fell in love with Barbara, a brunette. A short, stocky girl who reminded him of his mother, she had a nice smile and was very easy to get along with. She seemed to like everything he liked. She was sports oriented, they ran together and their sexual relationship was exceptionally good. Neither one of them was inhibited, so they tried sex in every conceivable position, reading *The Joy of Sex* together to stimulate their arousal. They were planning marriage after graduation.

Then, a blonde cheerleader type came along. Betty was not as bright or as easy to get along with as Barbara, but she was very pretty. She would not have sex with Jerome before they married. She had been taught that nice girls didn't like sex and guys didn't marry girls who "put out." It was not clear where that message had come from, but it was there and she lived by it, both before and after the marriage to Jerome. He broke up with Barbara, had a very short engagement with Betty and then married. On the honeymoon he realized he had made a mistake. Betty bored him and she didn't like sex. Although she tried, she could never get interested in it. She had spent too many years of turning herself off to control the men she dated.

Their sexual encounters were perfunctory with very little sex play because Betty was ticklish and really just wanted to get it over with. She encouraged Jerome to enter her before she was lubricated and then complained that it hurt. They conceived a child the first year they were married. Betty was a good mother and a good cook. She loved her baby and her husband. Their relationship was distant but she busied herself with homemaking, child rearing, and entertainment.

Externally, they looked and acted like a happy family, a facade they both chose to establish and maintain. They had the symbols but not the substance. There were many times when they both felt empty and alone. Neither one of them sought sex or romance outside the marriage: that did not fit with their value systems.

They acquired a great deal of material wealth and prominent status in the community. They were nice to each other but there was no romance, at least not in the chivalrous sense. Instead, there were obvious symbols, invested with exaggerated power, that held them together: their home, their wealth, their child, and their status in the community. *Is this a sad story or a happy one? You decide, it depends on your expectations and, perhaps, your value system.*

The symbol of the happy home, the functional family is invested with so much power that all of us are challenged to rationalize and delude ourselves about our own family members and relationships. Ideal families, black and white, are depicted on television sitcoms and commercials with regularity. Recognizing them as idealized does not mitigate the ill effects of the contrast with reality. A large part of the population is regularly distraught because they and their families do not measure up to the national ideal. This is particularly true during the holiday season, starting with Halloween and extending through New Years. Emphasis on family get togethers creates a pressure that results in a crisis season in counseling practices. People are more aware of their family identities during this time. If family dinners disintegrate into arguments, if mom and dad do not want to put their efforts into staging a family event yet one more time, or if adult children decide to stay home with their own young rather than make the traditional trip home for the holidays, there is a sense of loss.

Mom and Dad Clayton had four grown children and seven grandchildren under the age of twelve. They lived on a small farm close to Kansas City. The children were scattered in neighboring midwestern states.

Every year starting in October, family tension increased as everyone tried to decide how to allot holiday time among parents and grandparents. It was not a joyous process. In fact, Mom and Dad Clayton were worn out with hosting all the family functions. It was costly, energy draining and not very rewarding emotionally. But they were loathe to put an end to the tradition. Symbolically it meant they were old, unneeded and would die soon. These associations were shared by their children--who were also tired of packing up their own children for the long drive to Grandma's.

There was also the problem of how to apportion time between the families of origin of the two spouses. Tina, the oldest child, lived in Nebraska with her husband and two children. Her husband's parents lived nearby in the same town, so the opportunity to see them was always available. Tina felt guilty because she did not visit her own parents often. She was afraid that when they died she would regret not making more of an effort to see them. When she talked to her brothers and sisters over the phone, she discovered that they all felt the same way. This made her feel even worse. No one seemed to really love the folks. It was just duty and a sense of responsibility that motivated the annual get-togethers, but no one wanted to break with tradition.

Finally, Mom and Dad sent out an electrifying family letter. They were going to Arizona for the holidays and would not be able to host the family gatherings. This changed everything. Now the children would have to take individual responsibility if they were going to maintain an active relationship with their parents and each other. Mom and Dad were passing the torch. What would happen? Each person in the family felt older, and all the negative associations with aging came to the surface. There was also a feeling of relief and freedom. Now they could form their own traditions for their own families. What would happen to the folks? It was not much of an issue. They had outlived their usefulness. Now it was a matter of giving back, of children giving to parents, and the stereotype for this situation was even less clear than those governing the earlier phases of development in parent-child relationships.

Mom and Dad symbolized nurturance. They gave. The children received. There were a few platitudes about taking care of aging parents, but no one took the message seriously until they themselves were divested of their symbolic worth and faced the inevitable aging process. Associations with aging are usually negative, so the topic is avoided.

With consistent education regarding aging and its effect on family relationships, there can also be a sense of beginning, a new phase that holds its own romanticized symbols and stereotypes that appreciate rather than denigrate aging parents. There can be workable situations with guidelines for moving on to the next phase, but family mystique does not presently provide guidance for coping with the sequential stages of development. The association more often suggests nurturance for the young. It is not inclusive of care for the aging.

There are a multitude of family symbols and stereotypes that affect our view of ourselves. Every town or city has its old families or good families that dominate the social setting. These families as compared to what? New families or bad families?   Another leftover from medieval times, but impactful, nevertheless. The symbolism of the old family with old money beckons, evoking associations of power and riches, status and security. This is a general association, not a specific truth.

A member of an old family, even without money, still resonates with the symbolism of wealth and is sought after because of that general association. It is an empty symbolism, but it still has the power to evoke a complexity of conscious and unconscious associations that seduce and delude.

Gladys came from a "good family," an old family that for many generations had enjoyed an inherited wealth originally earned by a series of hardworking physicians, who earned more money than they could spend and had invested it wisely.   Intermarriage with other moneyed families had increased the family holdings, but as the generations went by, more money was spent than earned and the family values of hard work and stewardship fell by the wayside. By the time Gladys was in high school, everything was gone but the big house, the antiques, and the silver, which was still polished every week. It glistened symbolically in the palatial dining room where no meals were taken except on holidays or occasions when evoking the power of the past would be useful. Gladys and her mother, Sonia, ate their food in the family room or in their respective bedrooms while they watched television--no gracious living here. Nonetheless, they still hung tenaciously to the aura of wealth and status.

Sonia thought there was hope for her daughter, Gladys. She might marry well and somehow reestablish the family tradition somehow. There was no hope for Sonia. She had married Milton, Glady's father, hoping to better her own position as a middle class nurse. She soon was sadly disappointed. Milton turned out to be impoverished. He also had a drinking problem which kept him out of the way or inaccessible most of the time. He drank, gardened, and maintained the house to perfection, down to polishing the silver every week, but he earned no money. The only liquid assets the family had were earned by Sonia as a head nurse at the local hospital. The family kept their financial predicament a secret.

The townspeople thought Sonia worked as a nurse for altruistic purposes, a sign that she cared about people. They assumed she did not have to work because she had married well. That was the delusion the family sought to maintain by utilizing the symbols of wealth and grandeur. Sonia certainly had been seduced by those very symbols. The assumptions she had made about Milton were based on conscious and preconscious associations she had made with old families, old money, big houses, antiques, and gracious living. How ironic--Milton had been attracted to Sonia because she had a job, seemed independent and was very unlike the way he saw himself: dependent, unsuccessful, and nonproductive. He knew she was expecting more security from the marriage than she received. He knew he had seduced her with a delusion. It bothered him, when he let himself think about it, but he salved his conscience with alcohol and busied himself with mansion maintenance and silver polishing.

Their child, Gladys, was having trouble establishing her own value system. She liked expensive things and the symbolic status her father's family gave her, but there really wasn't much money so she did not fit in with her rich age mates. She had been exposed to the upper class ideal of nonproductive over consumption. She had been enculturated to expect a gracious life with little effort on her own part. When her expectations evaporated, she became bitter and disillusioned. Getting a job without marketable skills was difficult, if not impossible. Most important, it was embarrassing.

She did not really want to work anyway. She wanted someone to take care of her, to give her a big house and lots of money so she could enjoy a life without worry. Her expectations were unrealistic. The symbolism she had been surrounded with throughout her life had not completely clouded her perceptions. She knew she was poor and that her family was not powerful enough to help her achieve the exalted position for which she longed, but she could not give up the ideal. She was in danger of becoming a substance abuser, as her father had.

"I don't like to drink, it tastes bad, besides, it makes you fat. But pot is getting to be a habit for me." She sat there, peeling the nail polish off first one fingernail and then the next until there was a small pile of scrapings on her lap. "I need help and I hope you can help me."

It was clear that Gladys had to get her value system in line with her reality. She had to sort through her feelings she had about the conflicting life-styles to which she had been exposed. She knew she had to support herself or marry well. Neither option seemed acceptable. I asked her to explore her feelings about getting a job and taking care of herself. "I can't work at McDonalds," she said, "I'd have to move to another state. Everyone would laugh at me. I couldn't stand it." She cried freely, mopping her tears and her nose with tissues from one of the dispensers I always keep available in my office. She said the same thing over and over again in many different ways, crying continually. "I can't do it, I can't live that way, I can't be a nobody. I can't live in a ratty apartment. I can't sink to that level." Her anguish was genuine. She felt as if she had no life, no acceptable life. She might as well be dead or in jail as to be poor, self-supporting, and uncared for.

How had she come to believe that being poor was such a disgrace? Was it the example of her father? His maintenance of the family mansion as a shrine? His inability to adopt to a different life-style that he could provide for himself? Her mother's collusion in supporting the delusion seem to confirm for Gladys that the symbolism of the old family, the wealth, the status of the past was more important than real life and the present. The power of symbolism and the seduction of delusion had combined in this young woman's life in such a way that she truly could not see her existing options. Only the lost option, which was remote from anything she had ever really experienced, seemed viable.

During the course of her therapy, Gladys explored her belief system in depth. She was obsessed with the past--its glory, its extravagance, and what she imagined it was like to be one of the rich ones, one of the lucky ones, before her family lost its money. Since I could not pry her away from the past, I gave her the assignment of researching her family tree, utilizing the old therapeutic standby, the genealogical chart. Paradoxical intent. It was not long before she realized that the money in the dear, dead past had come from hard work. Her great, great-grandparents had worked hard as physicians. They had worked, saved, invested, and continued to work way past the point where others their age retired. The wealth they accumulated was more of a by-product of their labor than a goal in itself. This was not so for succeeding generations. Gladys remembered how her grandparents had flaunted their wealth, taking extravagant vacations and buying expensive cars. Her father had even learned to pilot a Lear jet. The family jet. They spent more than they earned, never focusing on the dwindling of the family resources. Her father never even tried to get a paying job. Gladys was judgmental at this point, blaming her parents for not bringing her up right and instilling her with better values. Blaming others is a dead end in therapy. I wanted her to focus on her responsibility to take control of her own life.

"You sound like you want to identify with the producers in your family rather than the consumers. Does that mean you're identifying with your great grandparents, the ones who worked so hard?" Gladys sat back and looked at me. She knew what I was doing--planting a suggestion. She pursed her lips and finally spoke, "I don't want to be like any of them." I nodded yes, "It sounds to me like you want to do it your own way." This time she nodded. Gladys began to identify with her great-grandparents, the ones she thought were hard workers. She seemed relieved to find someone she could respect from her search of family history.

Gladys continued to research her family, searching through the attic, basement, and closets of the family home. She was searching for a new identity. She put together some family albums and brought them in to share during session. The assembly process had given her a lot of time for focused thought. "They made a lot of mistakes," she said. "I wouldn't have spoiled my kids the way they did. They spent too much time working and not enough time teaching their kids how to work." It was interesting how she was no longer focusing on the material symbols representing wealth. She had switched her interest to the process of procuring wealth--working. Her grades improved and so did her spirits. Our sessions tapered off until we met every few months.

Had Gladys freed herself from the symbolism of the past?   Only partially. She decided on a premedical course in college and went on to medical school, certainly a family tradition. After graduation she moved to the Northwest. I do not know if she resurrected the past in a real or symbolic way in her own subsequent life, or whether it would have been healthy if she had. *What do you think? What is your experience with family symbolism? Recognizing your own romantic symbols and stereotypes increases our ability to form realistic relationships grounded in the present.*

Ed was forty-nine when his divorce was final. He had been married for thirty years to his high school sweetheart. One of their two children had grown and left home, and the other son was finishing his senior year in high school. Ed's marriage had been a happy one over at least twenty years, or at least he had felt it happy. His wife, Fran, was an attractive, vivacious woman who carried the responsibility for their social life and ran the home as well as holding a job as a librarian. Then she was diagnosed with cancer and became depressed. Her energy diminished and she quit her job. She was no longer interested in maintaining the family home. Instead, she watched television and sat for long hours alone, sometimes in the dark.

Ed, too, felt depressed. He started working late and involved himself in community activities to avoid being at home with Fran. She became angry at his neglect and filed for divorce. Ed was relieved; he wanted out. Feelings of disloyalty plagued him, especially when he was around his children (which was not very often). The children felt he had deserted their mother. In fact, his son had likened him to a rat deserting a sinking ship.

Ed struck up a relationship with a woman he met working on a committee for city planning. She was twenty-eight, very energetic and sexual. They had an exciting, torrid love affair which ended in an elopement to Las Vegas. Ed was very happy, he felt young again. His new wife, Grace, liked people and filled their house with parties and meetings. Quite a contrast with his life with Fran. They ate out a lot and enjoyed long weekend trips. It seemed like an endless courtship rather than marriage.

Then Grace became pregnant and announced that she wanted at least two more children. Ed was surprised and disappointed. They had never talked about children, except for some conversation about his will and a prenuptial agreement regarding his existing family. Everything was changing. The romance faded. The prospect of a new family overwhelmed him.

For Ed, Grace had symbolized a new life, a carefree, romantic departure from the depressing reaction to cancer that he had experienced with his first wife, Fran. For Grace, Ed had symbolized security and family. She wanted what all other women had, children and a home. She resented Ed's children from his first marriage, although she went through the motions of inviting them over for dinner and special occasions, it was clear they were not welcome to drop by without an invitation.

When Ed came to counseling to sort out his feelings, he felt that it was too late to turn back. He had married Grace based on the delusion that the flush of romance and excitement would last forever and make up for the ten years of unhappiness he had experienced in his previous marriage, with Fran. Grace had not lied to him, nor had he deliberately misrepresented himself. They had talked about the difference in their ages and what that might mean, but the mysticism of romance had clouded their perceptions.

Ed made an adjustment, but it was an unhappy one. He did not want to become a father again and share Grace's energy and attention with new dependents, but he felt trapped, and perhaps he was. Grace was not interested in counseling. She was afraid to dig too deeply in the circumstances of her life for fear of what she would find. But she did not prevent Ed from continuing with his sessions, which were focused on adjustment strategies for his new life with a second family. There were many times in session when Ed also felt he could not dig too deep or risk encountering his real feelings: guilt for leaving

Fran, grief caused by estrangement from his grown children, and resentment toward Grace for disappointing him, as well a lack of genuine interest in his new children. He was very disappointed in himself, as well as in Grace. He could not understand why he had failed to predict what would happen.

Another feeling Ed experienced was embarrassment: "I'm in the classic mid-life crisis. I feel like such a fool." Ed was not a fool. He was blinded by stereotypes and romantic symbolism, an association that can develop at any age whenever we are vulnerable. Our culture encourages us to think in terms of unsubstantiated symbols and stereotypes.

For Ed, a change of life circumstance had created anxiety and restlessness. He was afraid that he, like Fran, would become sick and die. So he succumbed to symbolism and built delusionary expectations around Grace. He regretted the end of his marriage. He regretted marrying Grace.

It is very likely that Ed would have made different choices had he been aware of his own feelings and associations. He would have been better able to cope with Fran's illness and depression if he had been systematically prepared for the normal course of events that occur in life development. Another example of how our educational system fails to meet a primary responsibility, that of preparing learners for the complexities of life and relationships.

Without adequate education, families are dependent upon unclear messages and poorly transmitted guidelines for living. Common sense and love are not always enough.

The Watson family had already endured a great deal of grief when Jack, the oldest son, announced he was HIV positive. Up to that point, the family claimed they had no knowledge of his homosexuality. He had lived on the West Coast, where he had a lucrative dental practice. He usually came home several times a year for holidays or when there was a family crisis. His parents had called Jack after his sister, Leah, had been killed in an automobile accident. The day after the funeral he had told the family members of his own crisis. They were totally shocked. They had difficulty focusing on his HIV condition, returning again and again to their disbelief that he was homosexual and to the death of his sister, Leah. The father, Gerald, just sat holding his head in his hands, saying; "You're gay? You're not gay! My own son, gay?" The mother, Diane, joined in the denial; "Why are you saying this? Why now? Your sister is dead. Can't you see we've had enough?"

Here we have a family made up of functioning, basically stable people with good values. There was an intact marriage of over twenty years and three grown children. None of the three children, however, had dated or married, which did not quite fit the stereotype.

The oldest son, Jack, was gay. He had never told anyone in the family about his sexual identity. Both parents had wondered why Jack didn't date women. Everyone in the family had pressured him fairly consistently about not being married. No one, however, had ever asked if he was gay or made any effort to communicate to him that he would be loved and accepted regardless of his sexual orientation. He finally relocated on the West Coast where there was a strong gay community that would furnish him with support for who he was. His family was still very important to him. He kept trying to maintain the illusion of belonging and being part of a family that knew and accepted him. He felt he needed that sense of family to function as an adult in the real world. His parents and siblings also valued family ties. They felt that their view, or their own stereotype of a family, was necessary for their sense of security. That view, of course, did not include a nonheterosexual member. The other children never dated, either. This may have been a kind of nonverbal, symbolic support for Jack, their oldest brother.

Fictional families such as the Brady Bunch or the Waltons do not allow an alternate life style or a member who is not heterosexual. Just think about it: 10 to 12 percent of the U.S. population, including readers of this book, represent variations of sexual identity that are never acknowledged in the mainstream culture as a positive choice. There are no mixed pink-and-blue ID bracelets in hospital nurseries. They are either pink or blue. Similarly, the Watson family could not acknowledge, even to themselves, the reality that one of their members, the oldest son, was homosexual.

In that time of crisis, after their daughter, Leah, had been killed in an accident, and Jack, the gay member of the Watson family, announced he was HIV positive, the family could not grieve adequately nor resolve their loss and integrate this pain. They could not support one another because the delusion of their family had been shattered. Their existing belief system was challenged. Confronted by a double crisis, they could no longer continue in their counterfeit roles. They had been role playing for too long. Authentic relating was unknown. It seemed mysterious and frightening. Their delusional roles were barely adequate to handle the crisis of Leah's accidental death. Combined with the revelation of Jack's homosexuality and his predictable death by AIDS, their roles utterly failed them. They were torn between wanting to maintain the delusional family stereotype or facing their dilemma. Unable to maintain denial and reimpose the stereotype, they were forced to redefine their roles based on reality as they now saw it. This relationship failure, as painful as it was, gave the Watson family the opportunity to emerge as real people in a real family.

What would you do if you were a member of the Watson Family? How would you feel? Would your belief system be flexible enough to accommodate new information that countered your existing family stereotype?

Stereotypes and romantic symbols to which we are exposed as children affect our behavior throughout our lives. In the mind of a small child, only the simplest categorical sorting process is possible. Broad associations thus occur in the undeveloped mind. When we attempt to teach a child about something as simple as masturbation, we risk also teaching that sex is bad, the private parts are bad, and touching the private parts is dirty. Parents and educators often believe that a child has understood and learned a message when that is not the case. John's father saw John masturbating. He sternly told his son to stop touching himself that way. John's father thought he had taught his son not to masturbate, but what John learned was that touching his penis was bad, erotic sensations were bad, and he himself was bad for having those feelings.

A child's mind is not sophisticated enough to distinguish between associational clusters. Thus, a consistent effort must be made to clarify associations that the child is forming. This can be accomplished by observing the child and listening to verbalizations the child makes about the information to which he or she has been exposed. It is simple to correct a misperception or overgeneralization. If as much time were devoted to clarifying ideas and associations about relationships and behaviors, sexual or otherwise, as is spent on teaching the multiplication tables and the ABCs, John's father would have handled the situation differently. If we can teach complex mathematical concepts with precision, we can teach a child that touching one's penis in front of others is not a socially approved behavior. John's father could have included clarifying comments that would teach John very specifically and clearly what the disapproval was connected to, thus avoiding overgeneralization and misassociations. Because we live in a sex-negative society, parents say too little, too fast, about sexual subjects, thus increasing the likelihood that a child will misunderstand the message and overreact to the emotion with which it is delivered.

Sometimes an overgeneralization process occurs that makes these maladaptive associations even more problematical. This happened to Reed, who was four years old when he started playing with a toy stove that had belonged to his older sister. He would place it on a little stool, sit in front of it, and pretend to bake cookies and cakes.

His older brother, Tom, was thirteen. Oftentimes their parents would pay Tom to babysit with Reed. During those times, Tom would invite Reed to play house, to be the mommy and submit to sexual stimulation of his genitals and anus. Reed did not know he was doing anything wrong. It was kept a secret, a kind of special activity between Reed and his older brother, Tom, whom Reed adored.

In a year or so, Tom outgrew the sex play and the memory of the activity receded into the past for both of them. The parents never knew, and the boys never talked about it. When Reed reached sexual maturity, he would often feel aroused in the kitchen of his home or when standing near a stove. After he married, he had difficulty with his arousal response, which was at its strongest when he saw his wife cooking or baking. He liked to fondle her as she was standing in front of the oven. This in itself is a fairly common male reaction as fondling a woman when she is engaged in typical female role behavior is a predictable outcome of gender-based conditioning. In Reed's case, however, the association was so strong that it reached fetish proportions. He was unable to feel arousal or achieve sexual satisfaction without the stimulus of the stove. His early childhood sexual experience with genital sensations linked his arousal response to the toy stove. They were then transferred to real stoves and, finally, to women near stoves.

It would have been equally possible for Reed to have established a homosexual arousal response, since his initial eroticism was associated with a male, his brother, Tom. This did not occur. However, the early association of eroticism with a toy stove created a symbolic link and the toy stove developed the power to arouse Reed. Later, an ordinary stove took on the same symbolic function, and eventually a stove had to be present for sexual excitement to occur. In its absence, Reed experienced erectile failure. What had happened to Reed was a chance occurrence in which the stove became a romantic and sexual symbol. Unlike the universal symbolism of the red rose or the gold band, the stove as a symbol was not culturally induced and transmitted purposely by educators in Reed's life. The experience illustrates, however, the lasting effects of childhood associations. Learning at certain developmental stages is powerful enough to be almost indelible. Strong emotions, which often accompany attraction and arousal, serve as bonding agents that invest symbols with the power to permanently alter our behavior.

Chapter 5

Awareness of Cultural Injunction

A child sits alone under a tree pondering the meaning of life. Today he heard that marriage was good and divorce was bad. No one really said that in so many words, but that was the message. Yesterday he heard that sex was bad and really quite funny. No one really said that in so many words, but that was the message. He also heard that Grandpa was dying. That was good because he was going to heaven and that was a great place to live. It was also bad, because when his life was over he would be put in the ground in a box and have dirt piled on top of him. No one really said very much about any of these things. It was confusing and scary. Where was a kid supposed to find out about stuff like this? Should he ask his parents, his teachers, the priest, or maybe go to the library or a computer, someplace he could get some answers?

The transmission of culture is intended as a benign process in support of custom and law. It becomes problematical when individuals and relationships are needlessly compressed into preexisting molds to facilitate homogeneity. A person's mental health status is affected by pressures to conform to cultural injunctions. Oftentimes, pressured individuals are believed to have mental disorders and are presented for treatment when it is the system itself that needs fixing. Many relationships and families are labeled dysfunctional when it would be more accurate to declare the cultural expectations of these systems rigid or obsolete.

The haphazard nature of the transmission process also contributes immeasurably to poor mental health. Take the parent-child relationship. Parents transmit in one set of messages and expectations. Children process the information, react to it, and then emit quite another set of beliefs and behaviors. This is a predictable outcome given the erratic nature of the process. Parents, however, are not usually educated to understand the transmission process. The results they see in their children are not clearly in line with their teachings. They become frustrated and believe that they have failed or that their children have failed when it is the expectations and the process that are at fault.

Very often, the process rights itself and the child exhibits a rough approximation of parental teaching that becomes even more refined with age. This also occurs in other cultural transmissions, like those between teacher and student.

There would be less need for contact with the mental health care system if our educational programs clarified the enculturation process: its purposes and limitations to learners in an ongoing way. Many of the problems listed in the V Codes of *The Diagnostic and Statistical Manual of Mental Disorders-IV (DSM-IV)* relative to conditions not attributed to a mental disorder could be eliminated through increased knowledge and awareness of cultural injunctions and how they affect relationships. The most salient point that could be made is that the cultural injunctions or rules are meant only as guidelines and need not be compulsively followed or rigidly enforced. This would reduce anxiety considerably in large portions of the population that take the guidelines too literally.

There is a classification called "Phase of Life," or "Other Life Circumstance" problems coded in the V Section of the *DSM-IV*. There is no underlying mental disorder in this condition, just a change in life circumstance, such as separating from parental control, marriage, divorce, retirement, or illness. In many of these cases, the underlying problem revolves around a misunderstanding of what is expected and a devaluation of self and relationship counterparts as a result. Very often, people report a vague sense of restlessness, anxiety, or failure in their relationships and they ask for confirmation of their perceptions regarding their rights and responsibilities.

Judy was twenty-two when she finished college with a degree in social work. Her mother had a Master's of Social Work (MSW) and encouraged her daughter to take the same career path. Judy was having trouble separating her identity from that of her mother. Her brother Jack, who was four years older than she, had experienced the same difficulty. He had majored in pharmacy and worked in the family drugstore after graduation. It was not until after he married that the family structure began to crumble, or at least that is how he saw it. They sat in my office, a twenty-two and a twenty-six year old, feeling uncertain about how to proceed. They were worried about how to break it to their parents that they wanted to live their own lives.

Jack spoke first, his speech was pressured; "It will break Dad's heart when he hears that I want to leave his business and try to make it on my own." "Your timing sucks," Judy said, "I'm moving to Baltimore." Judy's boyfriend had a job there and she had been planning to join him for over a year but had been unable to tell her parents because they had always assumed she would get her master's degree at the state university and settle in town nearby. The folks had even purchased several houses in the neighborhood for investment property that they intended to "give to the kids" when the time was right.

Jack and Judy were not interested in putting down permanent roots in their hometown, nor were they interested in their parents' money. It seemed like more of a burden than anything else. However, they felt guilty Judy more so than Jack. "There's always been a feeling that we'd all live and die here. The folks even bought a family plot with spots for us and our spouses. They've done so much for us, aren't we supposed to pay them back by hanging around until they die?" They both looked at me as if for an answer.

"How old do you figure you'll be before that happens?" I asked. There was a tense silence in the room, and then they both laughed. They got my point. It encouraged them to talk about their various options. Jack's suggestions were so ludicrous that I thought he was joking, "We can pack up and pull out in the middle of the night." I looked at him, maintaining my rule of silence when there was no obvious benefit from talking.

Judy knew he was not kidding: "Dad would have a heart attack. Remember what happened when you moved in with Crystal?" Jack nodded and yielded the point. I did not ask for clarification but got the feeling that there was some serious intergenerational "guilt tripping" going on. "What would happen if you just told them how you felt?"

Judy responded immediately: "They'd understand, say it was okay--even offer to help us--but inside they'd be bleeding. Mom would be devastated, and Dad might have a heart attack. He had one last summer and we've been walking on egg shells ever since. How can I think of leaving Mom when Dad's in such bad shape?"

Jack made another suggestion: "You stay, I'll go. That way they won't be left alone." Judy actually considered it this: "I guess I can call Jason and ask for one more year, but I don't think he'll buy it. He wanted me to go with him when he left eleven months ago."

Jack was beginning to sound desperate. "We've got to tell them and get on with our lives." They agreed to talk to their parents before their next appointment. When we met two weeks later, they had been unable to confront the issue directly with their parents. Jack, however, was beginning to communicate his feelings indirectly. He had not showed up for work at the pharmacy, nor had he called in. When his father went by his apartment, Jack had not responded to the doorbell. He did not answer the phone, either. What was going on? Jack was expressing his anger. He was also afraid of confronting his father. They were intelligent, responsible adults, yet they could not tell their parents how they felt. They seemed immobilized. They were trying to do the right thing. They loved and appreciated their parents, many messages throughout their childhood had left them confused regarding their responsibility.

I asked them to explore their feelings: guilt, fear, self- doubt, and anger. Anger at themselves, each other, and their parents. But the strongest feeling was one of paralysis. They simply could not act. Jack spoke of how his father had attended all his baseball games, coached his team, and been a really good dad, kind and generous. Judy agreed. She praised her mother for accomplishing much in her life and setting a good example for Judy: "She's never stood in my way--always understood." I felt like I was being fed a sugar-coated version of a make-believe family. "If they are so perfect, why do the two of you feel so trapped? Shouldn't they have taught you to be more independent?" They did not like my question, but I was not running for popularity queen. Perhaps I was becoming impatient. This case was dragging on and the issue seemed so trivial compared to some of the other cases I was carrying at the time. I really needed to bracket my feelings. Their pain was as genuine and deep as that of any other client. If they did not resolve it, their lives could be altered and restricted indefinitely. They had to set themselves free. Why was I not doing a better job? Why was it taking so long? A light went on: This was similar to an issue I was still grappling with in my own life. My grown children were in the process of reevaluating of their lives. One of the issues was their possible relocation. This awareness made it much easier to bracket my feelings and focus the sessions more clearly.

I was torn about suggesting a family meeting which might reinforce their inability to make life decisions independent of parental consent. They had not asked for family counseling. Their developmental task was to separate from the family system. They were lagging behind the developmental norm. A meeting with their parents seemed inappropriate, so I said nothing but continued to facilitate their discussions.

Then an interesting thing happened. They started to argue with one another in session, which gradually lessened the time they spent together outside of session. This had always seemed excessive to me, compared to most sister-brother dyads of that age. A loosening of their identification with the family of origin was occurring.

Judy finally called in and scheduled an individual session. She had made a decision: she was leaving and going to Baltimore to live with Jason, her boyfriend. She had no plans to contact either her parents or brother. I supported her decision. It was not direct or assertive behavior on her part, but it was movement. She hugged me and promised to keep in touch. When Jack discovered what she had done, he was relieved: "I'm telling the folks this weekend. By summer, I'm outta here." I nodded and smiled; he had transferred his need for symbolic parental approval to me. I would be quite a bit easier to dismiss than his parents.

Why had it been so difficult for this pair of siblings to accomplish the maturational task of separating from their parents? In their discussions, they had talked at length of the many profamily messages they had heard as children. Mom was fond of saying, "Blood is thicker than water," and, "The family that plays and prays together stays together." Dad was a genealogy buff. He had the family coat of arms framed and hung on the wall in his den. He also had one in his office at the drugstore and, of course, Jack was a junior named after his father and destined to inherit and inhabit his father's place. This was a tight family. The value of family loyalty had been consistently reinforced by the community and the larger culture. The transmission process had been an unbalanced one.

Jack and Judy had not received similar messages about autonomy and independence. They had also screened this type of message out because it conflicted with the larger value of family cohesiveness. This is a clear case in which exposure to consistent information on the life process and its maturational phases would have made a significant difference in the transmission of cultural injunctions. Jack and Judy, along with their parents, would have been more aware of the process and better prepared for their natural separation when it occurred.

Similar misunderstandings occur regularly in other phase of life areas. Marriage and divorce are significant phases in life. Cultural injunctions regarding what to expect are inadequate to prepare most people. Divorce rates would be reduced considerably if the basics of relating were regularly taught in all public and private schools. Natural processes, such as separation from the family of origin, and other life circumstance issues are important enough to be included in basic education curriculum.

Basic information on attraction and bonding would have benefitted Sandy and Bill. Sandy was very traditional. She wanted to have a large family and be a stay-at-home mom. Her religious beliefs supported that role, and she envisioned herself as being a beloved matriarch who was always there for her children. Her own mother had been very different: she had preferred to work and limit her childbearing. There were no siblings. Sandy did not feel that she had a home until she married Bill and had her children. She felt cheated because her childhood home life was not the ideal depicted in *Parents' Magazine*. Her decision to have a large family and be a full time homemaker was rooted in what she had experienced as childhood deprivation. One of the reasons why she was attracted to Bill was that he came from a large Catholic family that got together frequently to celebrate birthdays and holidays. She married him as much for what he seemed to represent as for who he was.

Bill was the third of five sons and felt somewhat lost among his siblings. His view of a large family was not as romantic as Sandy's. In fact, there were times when he had considered going into the priesthood because he disliked the hustle of family life. When he met Sandy, they quickly sexualized their relationship. They married because she was pregnant and neither felt that abortion was an option. Bill felt trapped. He felt guilty because he did not really love Sandy and would have preferred to remain single. His sexual urges had gotten him into trouble. He was not a happily married man, but his belief system did not include divorce, so he stayed and they had four more children.

What happened in Bill's life paralleled what had happened to his father. Since they did not have a close relationship, Bill was unaware of the similarity between himself and his father. There was not much talking or active transmission of ideas. When they did talk, it was very significant for Bill. He remembered his father telling him that doing the right thing was very important. Like being good to women, taking care of them, and supporting his children. That was important too. He couldn't be too selfish--family men have to give up a lot. Watching football was okay, and reading the paper, these were men's things. Women sometimes got upset about that, but it a trade-off, something you could do in exchange for giving up your freedom in life. Bill never quite understood how his father felt. He sensed a feeling of resignation, but Bill tried to be like his father, both consciously and unconsciously. But there were consequences. Bill felt pressure from within. Sometimes it scared him when he realized how much he identified with the offensive linemen while watching football on television. He wanted to knock the others down, hurt them, smash them. Once, while he was watching a play-off game, he threw his glass across the room, smashing it against the wall. It surprised him, startled his wife, and scared his children. How could a game be so important? How could it engender such strong feelings in Bill? He seemed to have hidden anger and a need to act it out. For the most part, however, he suppressed his feelings.

Sandy did not understand. She resented television, football, and even his reading the daily newspaper--anything that took his attention away from her and the children. She was so wrapped up in the family that it became everything to her. She wanted her husband to feel that way, too. Sandy did not realize that he was already sacrificing so much out of a sense of duty to her. Had she known, it would have made her angry. He was supposed to love her, but he did not. It was only sex that had brought them together. It made her feel insecure. She never felt important enough. Always afraid he would leave. So she had child after child, trying to bind them together with mutual responsibility. She did not like sex with him because he never kissed her. Kisses are romantic, they also felt good. Early in their relationship he would kiss her and she would feel sensations in her breasts and genitals. This never happened now. Sex was no longer enjoyable. He did not kiss her. It made her sad and angry, but she said nothing because she was so dependent and she knew sex was important to him. She was afraid she would hurt his feelings and make him feel less like a man because he couldn't make her feel good in bed.

Where did she get these ideas? Where did they come from? No one had ever told her that this was what a woman was supposed to feel. No one had ever told her what a man was supposed to be like. She assumed she was alone in her thoughts, that there was something wrong with her because she was not happy, even though she had what she had always wanted and was supposed to have, a husband and children.

It would have surprised her if she knew that Bill had many of the same feelings: unfulfilled sexual desires, restlessness, and dissatisfaction with his life. They were both resentful but concealed their feelings, as if they had no right to feel the way they did. Why didn't they talk about it, or try to make some kind of adjustment? No one had ever told them what they could expect of marriage, sex, or parenting--only that it happened. It was the normal course of events--but what is normal? Neither one knew. If only there had been a course in school, entitled "Relating 101," it would have helped. They would have known what to expect, what their options were, and what other people felt. Now it was too late--there was no turning back.

They both wondered if they were normal. They sought me out after a community presentation I had made on "Delusional Relationships." They wanted to know if their emptiness and gnawing unhappiness was something that everyone felt, and they wanted to know if their relationship was delusional. I believe that at the time, it was. They did not really know each other; they were unsure why they had stayed married. Their belief systems were confused. Both were intelligent people who wanted more from life, but they believed that there was something wrong with them, not the system. Each felt inadequate. Like they were not strong enough or smart enough to achieve contentment. Sandy blamed it on her childhood, some vague notion that she hadn't been loved enough. Bill believed that there had been too many children in his family of origin and not enough attention to go around. Their assumptions were partially true, but there was a more significant determinant involved. The educational system had failed them. Their culture had provided them with insufficient data on self-understanding. They had received no information on relating, except in the vaguest terms, like the Ten Commandments and the Golden Rule. They had been forced to fall back on what they picked up along the way from the models in their environment.

Sandy, because of her own experience of loneliness, had been determined to have a large family so she would never be alone again. How simplistic, but she did not realize it. She thought she had a plan that fit with what she could accomplish as a woman. Girl Scouts had given her a badge for embroidery and baking but had not mentioned romance or sex. What little she learned about those topics came from comic books and romance novels. She also saw a lot of movies and television. That is how she learned about life, marriage, parenting, and sexual communication. All the important things had been excluded from her educational process. She was taught how to read, write, add and subtract, and had a few classes in reproductive biology, but if it hadn't been for advice columnist Ann Landers, she never would have known that other people actually had similar problems and that there were ways to solve them.

Sandy, like many others, had also gotten the message that this kind of knowledge came naturally--that if you listened to your heart and used common sense, you could figure out what to do without any help or special education. She felt an abiding shame that she couldn't figure it out. Relationships, sex, parents, they all were supposed to come naturally. That had not happened. Her biggest problem was her feelings. She did not understand them. They made her behave irrationally. She snapped at her children and yelled at her husband. She saw herself as a bitch. She felt intense shame because she believed herself to be stupid and weak. That was how she saw herself--very different from the ideal woman she wanted to be.

The same was true for Bill. He had learned how to be a man from watching his father, his brothers, and other men in the neighborhood. He had also seen many priests, who had impressed him favorably. Their lives were orderly and peaceful. He assumed they were not plagued by sexual feelings. Bill also wished he could have played sports. He was an avid football fan like his father. He received the message that, as a man, he was supposed to be tough, strong, fast, and win, always win. There were not many wins in Bill's life. He wasn't very physical. The ideal image of men was physical--very physical. His exposure to the male stereotype had been very limited. One of his unfulfilled desires was that he wanted to cook. On occasion, when he was alone at home, he would watch a program that featured a chef. A man cooking. It really appealed to him. Bill didn't know why. Maybe because it was different, something men didn't normally do. The best thing about Sandy getting pregnant and having a baby was that he got to cook during her recovery period. He was not very good at it, but it was fun. In his heart he knew it was okay, but Sandy always made him feel that he was gay or something because he liked it so much. Like rear entry sex, Sandy had the idea that he had a gay streak because he liked to do it that way. She didn't say so directly but made several comments about it being unnatural, the way homosexuals did it. Bill never answered--he just felt funny and didn't try it that way very often.

Bill knew he had feelings that were not depicted as okay for men. The popular literature, newspapers, magazines, and paperbacks pretty much limited what a guy could think and feel if he wanted to fit in. Sandy and Bill both wanted to fit in. Neither had any desire to be a leader or a rebel. But they weren't clear on what they were supposed to do or be to fit in. Should they have been given more explicit information on the extent and limits of role behavior? If so, who should have been responsible for this--their parents, the school, the church? Would it result in even more control and confusion to include classes on understanding oneself and relating to others in kindergarten, elementary school, high school, and college, or should this continue to be left to chance? Leaving it to chance seems ineffective. Important life decisions require preparation. Men and women deserve to know what forces control their behavior. The force of ignorance controls much human behavior. Ignorance results from lack of awareness.

Marla's compliance to cultural injunctions gave her headaches. She also suffered from fatigue and irritability. It was not uncommon for her to explode in a rage at the slightest provocation. Once while applying makeup, she became so dissatisfied with the results that she smeared the mirror and walls with lipstick. She later had to remove the wallpaper and replace it. Marla was twenty-six when this occurred. She was very particular about her appearance and usually looked well groomed. There were times when she felt driven to achieve perfection, while there were other times when she didn't care and slouched around the house without makeup and wearing rumpled clothes, almost as if she were rebelling. However, she never went out looking that way. It was clearly difficult for her to meet the standards she set for herself regarding personal appearance.

Her husband, Barry, reassured her that she always looked pretty. Barry was very accepting. He seemed unconcerned when her anger flashed. He either tried to be understanding and empathic or avoided her until she cooled down. He believed that women were just that way at a certain time of the month. He also excused a lot on the basis that she didn't feel good. He never confronted her. His responses had been affected by the stereotype of the enduring husband who remained a nice guy even when things went wrong. He was not sure where he picked up that model for his behavior. His father had been alcoholic--anything but a nice guy, particularly under pressure.

As a child, Barry had been terrified of his father's rages. He remembered lying very still in bed, waiting for his father's anger to subside. As an adolescent, he had been keenly aware of other adult males who were calmer--men who controlled themselves. That's how he wanted to be. When he met Marla, he had already developed a "nice guy" image which he sought to maintain even when Marla was unreasonable. There were many times when she had temper tantrums. Barry prided himself on waiting them out. This had a negative impact on Marla's behavior and their relationship. Marla took his patience and forbearance as approval of her immature outbursts. Since he did not challenge her or end the relationship, she developed a sense of entitlement to her fits of rage. The problem was never clarified or resolved. They unwittingly colluded to maintain this pattern of interaction.

Marla did not realize how angry she was. She felt it took a good deal of energy to survive. She was always hungry because she was afraid of getting fat. She dieted incessantly to maintain the image of slimness. She rarely ate a full meal, relying on breath mints and diet sodas for energy. She exercised conscientiously to avoid getting flabby. She also spent many hours on wardrobe maintenance and grooming. She wore a lot of makeup but achieved a natural look by studying cosmetic advertisements and reading magazine articles on feminine beauty. Marla frequently kept Barry waiting while she changed her outfit several times. She felt driven to look her best, which meant slim, firm, pretty and well dressed.

She also wanted to do all the right things that successful women did, but she wasn't quite sure how to accomplish that. Marla, like many other women, absorbed bits and pieces of various messages and stereotypes and attempted to fashion her own model for being a woman. Since much of this was done on a preconscious level, she had little awareness of how delusional and rigid some of her beliefs were. Like the idea that it was all right for her to lose her temper and behave irrationally. She had always heard that women were bitches. This may have served as some kind of self-fulfilling prophecy. There were also many jokes about screaming, carping women, and she had absorbed the idea that it was normal. Premenstrual Syndrome (PMS) got so much press, negative as it was, that she felt entitled to bad days when she could vent her negative feelings. The culture seemed to be giving her permission to lose control and be abusive to others. There was an international female stereotype for this behavior. Had Marla succumbed to it without awareness? She did not like herself for behaving that way, as it engendered guilt. Marla was aware of another cultural pattern for her behavior--the smiling, pleasant, compliant pattern which required what felt like superhuman control and self-sacrifice. Marla really wanted to be that kind of woman, but she could not. Her headaches, her tension, and her anger came from dissatisfaction with her inability to meet these various ideals, but she kept on trying, even though it made her miserable. Marla had very little insight into her predicament. She felt only a vague awareness of what she was doing. No one seemed to understand except for Barry, and they never talked about it, perhaps because they did not fully understand their own feelings and behaviors.

Barry had even less awareness. And he was happier. The world was less critical of nice guys than of angry women. Barry also struggled with cultural expectations. He did not want a nine-to-five job, or to wear a shirt and tie. He thought men looked ridiculous dressed that way. He also did not want to be a major provider. One of the reasons why he felt attracted to Marla was that she was self-sufficient and didn't need his financial support. It didn't seem to bother her that he lacked steady employment. He odd jobbed it. Earning money by doing painting, carpentry, lawn maintenance, and anything he could find to pay his share of the bills. He liked to write. He had about four unfinished novels going. He had also written some short stories and lots of poetry, but he did not try to sell his work. Perhaps he was afraid of the rejection involved in finding a publisher. Marla told her parents and friends that he was an author, not because she cared about his status but because she did not want to deal with their snobbery. She was responding to the cultural injunction that a man should have a good job and that a woman who can not find a man with a good job is less than adequate. This particular cultural injunction was well within Marla's awareness, but it involved Barry, not her. She did, however, want to avoid parental disapproval, so she complied with a mild form of deception and referred to him as an author or poet. He was really a handyman.

Barry's response was more complex. He felt he was complying with the cultural injunction to work and provide for his woman. His income paid almost half the bills, and he provided for Marla in other ways. He washed her car and filled it with gas. He rubbed her back and brought her tea in the morning. They had an understanding. He felt no conscious anxiety regarding his nontraditional blue-collar status as a worker. At a deeper level, however, Barry felt self doubt because he was unable to meet the cultural injunction to be major provider. This was linked to his father's alcoholism. Barry had felt less than other boys who had not been handicapped by a father who drank. He felt he could not measure up. Barry himself rarely drank and felt uncomfortable around others who did. He preferred to be alone or with a woman rather than in the company of men. He was not aware of feeling inadequate, just felt uncomfortable because he knew he was different. His nice guy demeanor was not a pose, but it served as an effective defense against competing with other males. If he didn't get angry, he didn't have to fight or test himself. Perhaps he felt afraid that he couldn't pass the test. There were so many tests for men. Barry did not want to try. He was unmotivated, but people liked him. He was cheerful and nonthreatening; nice to be around.

Generally, he felt happy. Even though he was not striving to meet cultural expectations, he was at peace with himself. Marla's acceptance of him gave him confidence. The temper tantrums did not drive him away because she never directly criticized him. Besides, her outbursts were irrational, so he could not take them seriously. They did not threaten his viability as a man.

Barry and Marla were a fairly good match. They accepted one another. She did not try to force him into compliance with cultural injunctions, gender based or otherwise, while intuitively, he understood her unhappiness as the result of her high level of compliance to the cultural injunctions she perceived. It validated his stance of noncompliance. Marla appreciated his tacit acceptance of her rages. He seemed to understand her struggle to do everything right and how it unnerved her. Even though Marla lacked insight into her own compliance, she definitely respected Barry for his noncompliance with cultural expectations. She wished she could be more like him. He admired her and wished he had some of her qualities. Marla and Barry balanced cultural expectations with their own abilities. They might be judged as well adjusted or dysfunctional. How would you judge their adjustment to cultural pressures?

How would you evaluate their level of awareness? Compare it to your own?

A cultural injunction is a pattern for appearance and behavior. Resulting from years of tradition, it governs expectations of ourselves and others. It functions as a standard against which relationships are measured. If we choose to comply with a cultural standard, we should at least know it is there and understand what it means.

Chapter 6

Forcing the Relationship Back into the Stereotype

You are in the process of making a difficult decision. It involves the fate of an unborn child that you and your lover have conceived out of wedlock. Your choices are to abort the child, have the child and arrange to have it adopted, have the child and raise it out of wedlock, or you can marry to protect the child from illegitimate status and then divorce, since you do not feel that your lover would be suitable as your life mate. Or marry and stay together for the sake of the child.

If you are female, you also have the option of not informing your lover that you are pregnant. You would then make all decisions and take all responsibility yourself. If you are male, you have the option of contesting paternity, forcing your lover to take you to court to secure your contribution to the child's support and the expense of childbearing and/or adoption proceedings.

You feel confused and uncertain about the process you are going through. You want some help, but you are very ashamed to find yourself in this position. Who would you choose to talk to? What kind of help would you want? Is there someone in your life to whom you would turn in this situation?

Let's look at how one person handled it. Ellise decided to tell her parents. She was twenty seven years old. Her parents had always respected her choices in the past, so she felt safe in seeking their support. They were not immediately supportive. They expressed disappointment and shock. Their first reaction was to encourage her to marry the father. They had never met him and were disturbed to discover that Ellise did not like him and had no intention of marrying him. "He is okay to date," she said, "someone to have a good time with, but I don't respect him and can't see myself parenting a child with him.

What I know about his family makes me feel certain I would not want any child of mine being influenced by them. The child would be better off adopted. At least there would be two decent parents."

Ellise's parents then encouraged her to have an abortion, saying that it would be difficult for her to carry the baby to term without everyone knowing about it. Eventually, Ellise lost her temper, telling her parents they were being callous and insensitive and that it was hard enough for her to make up her mind without pressure from them. This was uncharacteristic of her as she was not an assertive person.

During session she would lie on the couch and cry because her parents were more concerned with their image in the community than they were with her feelings. She felt judged by them. Ellise was in a regressed state. She wanted unconditional love and support from her parents, which, of course, was impossible. Naturally, they had their own view of the world, and their value systems were obviously different from that of their daughter. Their first thoughts, when they learned of the pregnancy, involved trying to make it fit into their world with minimal disruption. This infuriated Ellise. She wanted, even demanded, that they abdicate their position as independent adults and take on the role of her parents once more. She did not, of course, realize the extent to which she was forcing them into the parental stereotype. That was not an issue for her. Only her feelings and her predicament concerned her. It was clear that her expectations and behavior cued their parental responses and they temporarily regressed along with her, thus legitimizing her position as a helpless child.

Ellise confronted her parents angrily, crying hysterically until they began to feel guilty and changed their position to one of unconditional support regardless of what Ellise decided to do. They were even willing to adopt the child themselves so Ellise would not have to part with her baby nor have to assume the primary responsibility. They truly wanted to be helpful, but Ellise experienced their offer as unwelcome pressure. "They want me to be a dutiful daughter--either marry a guy I don't love or find some way to deal with the baby so they won't be embarrassed and the family won't be compromised." She was vehement: "It's a little late for that. I've let everyone down and they want me to know it. I feel so guilty. What shall I do?" She cried, shaking uncontrollably. The tears were streaming down her face along with her mascara. She caught a glimpse of herself in my office mirror and did not like what she saw. The shape of her body was already changing, which scared her. She was overwhelmed with conflict. There were too many options and she did not like any of them.

The only decision she had made was not to have an abortion. She did not want to keep the baby fearing it would alter the course of her life irrevocably. She wanted to maintain her career path and perhaps return to school for graduate training, but she was haunted by the fear of giving her baby away and then regretting it for the rest of her life.

"I can't bear to think of my baby wondering why I didn't love it enough to keep it, but how do you tell a child that it is illegitimate? The child would never respect me." She looked at me, pleading for some kind of comfort. I resisted the urge to reassure her that it would be all right, even though I knew that this was what she wanted to hear. Instead, I responded: "Your expressiveness is healthy. You are doing a good job of looking at all your options and trying to determine which is best for you." My response was designed to clarify that she was competent and capable of making a good decision for herself. She drew minimal comfort from that, but was able to refocus: "My feelings don't really matter. I've gotten myself into a mess and I've got to find my own way out." She looked at me and added: "I can trust you. You don't tell me what to do and you don't pretend there's going to be a happy ending. It helps ground me." She needed grounding as her natural tendency was to become hysterical and dependent.

Ellise did have options. She had interviewed with an adoption program that offered to pay for her medical bills, counseling fees, and legal advice. She could also participate in the selection of the adoptive parents. She spoke of was a process called open adoption, whereby she could see photographs of her child periodically. She pondered the advantages of open or closed adoption, but still could not resign herself to giving up the child. By her sixth month she had decided to keep her baby and become a single mother. "I feel so scared," she said. "Everyone will think I'm being selfish. The baby would have a much better life with two parents than one. And I still don't know how I'm going to tell him he's illegitimate. Do you think he will be totally messed up knowing the truth?" She wanted me to say no, but unrealistic reassurance was not in order.

"It's an issue. It might depend on whether you're at peace with your decision or not. Sometimes a child will sense anxiety. When you come to terms with your own feelings, you will be better able to help your child gain understanding and acceptance." Ellise replied, "It's not going to be easy, no matter what." I looked at her and nodded in affirmation.

Stark reality and unadorned truth had a calming effect on her. She seemed to feel stronger by just facing the problem, rather than sugar-coating it or overreacting to it.

Ellise's greatest problem throughout the entire experience involved forcing herself into what she saw as the conventional stereotype. She was not having her baby under conventional circumstances, so she was having difficulties seeing herself as a mother. She had difficulty seeing her child growing up without a father. When she thought about childhood, she thought in terms of two parents, a father and a mother, preferably birth parents. She knew of no models or acceptable alternatives for the circumstances in which she found herself. There was no existing model. She had to somehow give up the baby if she was going to fit the stereotype of a single woman. Single career women were not depicted as mothers. But she had other values she had to consider. She could not abort the baby, it was too late for that. Although she had never seen herself as prolife, she had so many negative associations with abortion that it was not really an option for her. The remaining option, which she had originally rejected, marrying the father began to look better to her. It represented the best of all possible stereotypes--the married, two-parent family. Her parents and the community would feel fine about it. The fact that the child was born only three months after the marriage would recede into the past. It was a minuscule point. No one ever focused on that, except maybe the child, at some distant future point when it would not be a primary concern.

Ellise scheduled an appointment with the baby's father, and they met in my office to talk about getting married. Craig, the child's father, spoke first: "I think we should put the baby up for adoption and get on with our lives. But if Ellise is going to keep it, we should get married and see how it works out." Ellise flushed; she was furious. At that moment he represented everything about the stereotype that she abhorred. "I don't want a shotgun wedding. People should not marry unless they love each other." Disgusted, Craig shook his head and grimaced. "I don't want a shotgun wedding either, but that's what we've got. You've blown the only other option we had, abortion. It's too late for that now. I don't want any kid of mine growing up illegitimate, especially in the community I live and work in. We've got to think of someone else besides ourselves here." Ellise had many of the same feelings but since Craig was articulating them, she was free to verbalize the other side of the conflict they both felt. "Just because we made a mistake and got caught doesn't mean we don't have a right to our own lives. I'm trying to do the right thing, but I don't want to be a living sacrifice. Besides, it's not such a good thing for a child to grow up in a loveless marriage."

"Ellise, we don't have to be in love. We could be friends and do a pretty good job of giving this kid a start. If we divorce later, at least he'll have a name and two parents that care about him. And we might make it. Lots of people that marry aren't madly in love."

Ellise looked at him silently. What he said seemed to make sense to her. She was wearing down. She looked at me and asked for my opinion. I didn't want to be in the position of giving advice or making the decision for her, so I dodged the question and commented on their process. "Craig, you're focusing on problem solving. Ellise is still trying to sort through her feelings, so she isn't as able to make a final decision as you seem to be."

Craig flushed, "I'm not allowed to make any decisions. Ellise is making all the decisions. I just get to pay for it."

Ellise started to speak, coughed instead, and glared at both of us. "I'm paying for it too. This is my body, remember? You're not the one with aching feet and a sore back. The only decisions you're ready to make involve killing the baby or giving it away. If those are the kinds of decisions you're going to make, you won't be making them about me or my baby!" By this time, her voice had risen and she was yelling. She then started to cough again. Suddenly the room was silent. Craig poured her a glass of water from the pitcher on my desk and Ellise took the glass and drank the water. It seemed like a significant interchange.

Ellise continued, she was relieved to be given the opportunity to express her feelings. "Not only will I miss time at work just having the baby, but as the mother, I'm the presumptive parent. It will be me, not him, that they call if something goes wrong at day care or school." Again the room fell silent. The enormity of the changes necessary to keep the child were beginning to sink in. Craig got up and walked over to the window. Looking out with his back toward us, he said, "I can work at home, some of the time. I'm not a selfish son of a bitch. I'll do my share." His voice was tense. Looking at Ellise he said, "We did the crime, we do the time." She said, "You make me sick. That's a terrible way to see a baby. A new life should be something everyone is happy about. Getting pregnant is not a crime." She started to cry and he tried to comfort her, saying, "I didn't mean it that way." She stiffened and did not respond.

Craig had offered comfort and Ellise had refused it. I said, "Ellise, how did you feel when Craig said that?" The words rushed out of her mouth. "Like he's trying to get to me. Again. Like he did before he screwed me. Trying to act like a nice guy. So he can get his way. Everything he says and does is for himself. It makes me so mad!"

Glaring at him, she picked up her purse. I thought she was going to throw it at him. He did, too. "Go ahead, if it will make you feel better. Hit me. You are acting like a spoiled brat yourself."

My own feelings were moving. It would not have been the first time a physical conflict broke out in my office. I was getting tired and was not anxious for another pitched battle. I wanted to establish a more productive process without squelching their feelings. "I'd rather you talked about it. Sounds like you feel exploited, Ellise."

It worked. She put her purse down on the couch next to her and began to talk. It was very productive. They were both angry and disgusted with the way the other person was behaving. Neither had fully expressed their feelings. They did so in the remainder of that session and were able to temporarily resolve their relationship.

They decided to marry. Ellise was very doubtful. "I think I'd feel better if I had my baby alone and raised it myself, without any input from anyone else. I'd feel stronger; as if I had accomplished something for myself. This way I feel like I've given up. I hope I feel differently later."

We continued to meet for four months after the baby was born. They seemed to be developing a friendly, affectionate relationship. As far as I know, they are still together.

How would you feel if you had this decision to make? Would you force yourself into a stereotype or choose another way, even if it were harder? Is it appropriate for people to exercise choice regarding the extent to which they impose a stereotype upon their relationships? Ellise and Craig decided together, consciously, to be governed by an existing pattern for their relationship. They were certainly aware that their circumstances did not fit the norm, but together, they made a choice to adjust their relationship to meet stereotypic expectations. They were able to cooperate because it was a joint decision.

When one partner attempts to force a relationship into a stereotype without the consent of the other, emotional blackmail occurs. Guilt, bribery, and threats are frequently used to establish stereotypic guidelines for behavior in relationships. This may not occur with conscious intent. In fact, the person doing it may not fully realize what is occurring.

Bernard came to my office seeking help in getting his wife, Emily, to become more sexual. She disliked having sex with him and did everything she could to avoid it; staying up late, not bathing before coming to bed, and discussing other problems in the bedroom so their mood would not be conducive to sexual encounter. Bernard was frustrated. No matter how he expressed his feelings, Emily rejected his advances. He finally decided to leave the relationship in hopes of forcing his wife to comply with the changes he wanted.

He was a successful businessman and provided a comfortable life for them. Emily did not work outside the home. Except for teaching piano to a few neighborhood children, she was completely financially dependent on Bernard's income to maintain the standard of living she enjoyed. This gave him a lot of power, which he had never tried to use to his advantage before. What he hoped to accomplish by leaving was to scare Emily into changing her behavior: "I don't want a divorce or any other woman. I just want a normal relationship with my wife."

Emily was scared when she came in for her individual session. She said, "I feel like I have to greet him at the door in a red lace nightgown or I'm out with the trash." She was also very angry. "We were doing okay until he got this idea that he could make me jump through hoops." "Okay?" I queried. She went on to describe a sexual relationship very different than the one Bernard had described.

I was not surprised. Spousal perceptions of their sexual relationship differ markedly. It is rare for a husband and wife to agree on factors like frequency, initiation, or length of sex play when they are describing their relationship. I usually just listen and then ask them each to describe in joint session what they want from each other sexually.

Bernard wanted more affection, more attention, and more variation in their sex lives. He also wanted Emily to pursue him, take the initiative, and make him feel wanted. He felt she should use perfume, dress up for him, and take responsibility for arousing him when he was tired.

Emily felt that this was not normal: men were supposed to take the initiative. She felt that her husband should be aroused by her in a natural state and not expect her to take responsibility for his waning sex drive. "I don't want to objectify myself because he can't respond to a woman in her normal state."

Bernard was embarrassed when he heard Emily's version of their sexual relationship. It was true that his erections were not as firm as they once were and he now experienced delayed ejaculation. Sometimes he could not ejaculate at all, regardless of how much stimulation he received. With this information out in the open, it was difficult for him to maintain the delusion that Emily was solely responsible for the problems in their sexual relationship.

As we talked, it appeared that Bernard met the criteria for a second classification, Inhibited Sexual Excitement, as well as that of Inhibited Male Orgasm. After consulting a urologist, it was ascertained that Bernard's condition was not exclusively caused by organic factors, which meant that Bernard had a psychosexual dysfunction.

For years Emily had accepted responsibility for his condition because she did not fit the sex kitten stereotype. They had colluded in blaming her for his problem. At the outset of counseling, Emily did not fully disclose the extent of Bernard's problem. She was protecting him. But as our joint sessions continued they were both more able to describe their relationship without defensiveness.

Bernard said he had always felt inadequate because his sex drive was not as strong as that of other guys. He had never felt the urge to masturbate during his teen years. He enjoyed sex but it was not a primary concern. Emily's disinterest in sex seemed to parallel his, so it worked out well until he turned forty and began to feel as if he were getting old and missing something. Since Emily did not fit the *Playboy* centerfold image, it was easy for him to focus on that rather than his own sexual inhibition. His presenting problem was his wife's disinterest in sex. His initial plan was to enlist my support in forcing her into the female stereotype.

This was not done on a fully conscious level. In his heart, Bernard knew that he had the problem. His defense was to use a cultural stereotype, which placed all responsibility on the woman to excite her man. He expected Emily to remain attractive and meet his needs at the expense of her own. He felt justified in trying to force her to change rather than accepting the problem as his own and making the necessary changes in himself.

Bernard was afraid to look at himself too closely. He had been subjected to another common sexual stereotype that described the male as very sexual, always ready, and not at all inhibited. If he examined himself too closely it would become crystal clear that he was not the stereotypic male. The feelings of inadequacy were hard to bear. It was easier for him to depict Emily as falling short of the sexual ideal for a woman and evade responsibility.

Once this basic issue had been clarified and understood, Bernard and Emily were able to make a realistic assessment of their sexual relationship. They focused more on nonerotic encounters and engaging in more cuddling and kissing. Paradoxically, this type of contact had the effect of increasing their arousal response.

Their encounters did become more erotic and satisfying once they stopped trying to force themselves and their relationship into a stereotype. It is ironic that the stereotype was not appealing to either one of them. Once their anxiety decreased, they were able to acknowledge this truth.   Appreciation and acceptance quickly followed.

The expectations that Bernard and Emily had of themselves can be traced to vague, but persistent, messages regarding what their sexual relationship should be like. When they realized that they did not have to entirely conform to the stereotype, they felt an overwhelming sense of relief. This made it possible for them to examine their differences without defensiveness and apply their energy to resolving their mutual problems. Prior to reaching that insight, they had expended a great deal of time and energy forcing their relationship into stereotypes. What a waste! Unfortunately, their struggle is paralleled to some degree in all relationships. Forcing a relationship into a delusive stereotype generates pain and confusion.

Let's look at a father-son relationship. Hank was ashamed of his father. He was poor, uneducated, wore overalls, had rotting teeth that smelled bad. The family farm on which he worked had always been marginal, and although there was usually food of some kind, it was plain and unappetizing. Hank's father, Robert, seemed pleased with himself because he provided minimal shelter, food, and clothing for the family. To Hank, this contrasted sharply with what other fathers provided for their sons. Hank was keenly aware of the paltry nature of the house in which he lived, the clothes he wore, and the food he ate. His classmates and neighbors all had more. Hank could not understand how his father could sit contentedly on the porch, tilted back on his wooden chair with a smile on his face, when other fathers were out earning money to provide for their families.

A dramatic incident occurred when Hank was thirteen years old. He wanted a bicycle; everyone else had one. He needed it to ride down the dusty roads to get to school and town. A bike would cost a lot of money. His father didn't have it, couldn't get it, wouldn't have spent it that way if he had it. Hank argued with his father, called him names and belittled him for what he thought he was: a poor, weak, sorry excuse for a man who could not provide the bare essentials for his son. Robert, the father, was first dismayed and then angry, filled with rage and hurt. How could his son talk to him that way? How could he be so ungrateful? Robert wanted to kill him. He regretted siring him. He wanted him gone.

Looking into his son's eyes, he didn't see the hurt, confusion, disappointment, or pain that Hank felt. He saw only anger and greed. It did not fit what a son was supposed to be like. Robert could not believe his own flesh and blood, his child, could turn on him this way, and for what?--a bicycle. What about everything else he had given his son: a home, food, clothes, a chance at an education? All things Robert had never been given. Robert had been proud of himself as a father and felt good about what he had accomplished as a provider, but now the image he had of himself was shattered. He saw it all differently. His son had turned on him and called him a failure. How had it all happened?

Robert had surpassed what he had expected of himself and had accomplished far more than his father before him. Unlike his own father, he had stayed and worked and hung onto the land so he would have something to pass on to his son, Hank--Hank, who hated him and held him in contempt. Robert felt sick. His stomach turned, there was a lump in his throat, and his eyes burned. He shook his head: how could this have happened? He had done the right thing. He had been faithful to Hank's mother, his wife, even though she had a sharp tongue and could be difficult. He had resisted the siren call of the bars. Unlike his father, he had turned his back on drinking and womanizing and had always put his family first. He never bought himself clothes or saw a dentist even though at times his head ached from the pain of his abscessed teeth. His wife wrinkled her nose at the smell and his son shamed him for how he looked and what he was.

How unfair. He felt like choking. Was his success a fantasy? Did no one see him as he really was? His son had betrayed him. God, he hurt--but no one knew he hurt. Robert never told. That would be against the rules for being a man. John Wayne would never tell. Suffer in silence, be a man, don't cry, act like you don't care. Be a cool dude.

Hank didn't know his father. He thought he was a strange, smelly old man who did not care--but that was not the case. Robert did care very much about being a man and doing the right thing. He followed the rules as he understood them. Unfortunately, he and his son, Hank, had different expectations of what a father should be.

As Hank went through the process of comparing his father unfavorably to his cultural stereotype of what a man and a father should be, he failed to notice any of his father's strengths or positive qualities. They never talked about feelings or even acknowledged them, except for anger. Both vented anger. It was like a channel through which all other feelings flowed. Shame, fear, guilt, all came out as anger, the approved feeling for men. That was how they saw it. To express other feelings was against the rules for being a man. Both Hank and his father, Robert, before him had picked up distorted messages concerning male identity from the culture. Their perceptions were different because of the differences in their ages and the subsequent variations in popular images that were purveyed by the media. Although there were many similarities in what they learned about how men were supposed to be, such as the proscription against feelings, there seemed to be more differences than similarities. This magnification of differences occurs because delusional relationships contain an emotional charge that increases during times of stress.

The conflict between Hank and his father is an example of magnified differences. Hank thought a bicycle was a necessity. His father, Robert, did not. But they did agree on the fact that the father should provide for the son. This basic agreement on the father's responsibility as a provider and that Robert had complied with that role requirement was lost in the blur of differing expectations and poor communication.

Hank was struggling with his own male identity. If he didn't have a bicycle he wasn't as good, in some way, as the guys who rode bicycles. He lacked something--a sense of his own maleness, the core of his identity, which was symbolized externally by the bicycle. He did not have the awareness or the communication skills to say to his father: "Help me to be a man. I'm not making it. My buddies are stronger and more male than me. Help me. I can't do it alone." Instead, he attacked his father, calling him names and ridiculing him. This was the male way, or so he thought. Show no weakness, demand what you want, look mean, and talk loudly. These were the confused messages that gave rise to Hank's angry confrontation of his father.

If Robert, the father, had grasped the true meaning of his son's message, he might have been moved to respond differently. He wanted to help his son be a man. He wanted his son to turn to him for help. Ironically, the two were on the same wave length. But they both lacked awareness and communication skills to express feelings other than anger. So they argued and the relationship faltered.

Was Robert a failure? Was Hank selfish? What have you expected of your own father? What do you know of what your father--or your son--really feel?

There are numerous stereotypes for males, many of which conflict. Sometimes men go from one stereotype to another trying to find themselves. Working stereotypes are formed by bits and pieces of illusive and idealized images and held in place by delusional thinking.

Brad measured his competence as a male by the profit margin of his business ventures and his sexual success with women. Sexual success for Brad was preconsciously linked to "scoring" in high school. It meant having sex with a girl whether or not she wanted or enjoyed it. It was exciting and satisfying for him to handle a woman's breasts and genitals roughly. He liked to say the word "cunt" during sexual encounters to increase his arousal. All this was without apparent awareness or concern of how it felt to the woman. Brad was complying with a male stereotype. Much of the excitement came from the fantasy that he was needed so badly that he could do whatever he wanted. It involved feelings of power, control, and dominance.

He was embarrassed and angry when Tracy, his second wife, moved out of the bedroom, saying she felt degraded and abused, and that she was no longer interested in being his sexual partner. "I thought women liked that," he said, "Why didn't she tell me sooner?" Tracy said she had not told him sooner because she knew it would make him angry and he might seek sexual satisfaction outside of the marriage. She had been trained to protect a man's ego and avoid telling him the truth. He couldn't handle it. How did Brad actually react to the truth? He was outraged and demanded the right to show her he could please her sexually.

He really wanted to do it, but when given the opportunity, he grew tired of kissing her or trying to caress her in just the right way to prepare her for penetration and thrusting. He lost interest in sexualizing with her and avoided sexual encounters with her. The truth was that his arousal reaction diminished and disappeared when he had to curb his own feelings and behaviors to meet her sexual needs. He no longer felt like a man. He had been told that women would love him just for being a man, whatever that meant. For him, as with many males, good sex meant domination and power, not tenderness and mutual satisfaction. The epitome of masculinity was to be powerful enough to have what he wanted regardless of the cost to others. This was true in sex and business alike.

Brad was a prisoner of a male stereotype, but he didn't realize it until after his second marriage was over. It was only after he had been in therapy that he began to gain insight into his own behavior. He was, in many ways, a stereotypic male. "But is that bad?" he would ask, and then, answering his own question: "Of course it's bad if Tracy doesn't like it. But, what's a guy supposed to do? Maybe he needs to go somewhere where he can be a man and not worry about hurting a woman's feelings or injuring her body." But he knew that this would work only as long as he kept it a secret from his wife. Tracy would divorce him, or worse, do the same and cheat on him.

He feared that he was sexually inadequate; that he could not meet the standards or requirements for being male. To reassure himself, Brad developed the habit of automatically assuming male role behaviors whenever he was in the presence of a woman, particularly a woman who gave off signals of being stereotypically female. He assumed the demeanor of a man on the make. He would talk, direct his attention, give compliments, and even offer to do little favors for casual female acquaintances or business associates--the type of thing men usually do grudgingly for their wives or girlfriends. He had little awareness or concern for how inappropriate his behavior was or how it impacted on others. Tracy was embarrassed by his conduct in social situations. It was hard for them to make friends. Other couples did not seek out their company because it had a negative effect on their own relationship. Many of Brad's clients also took their business elsewhere because of these behaviors.

It was unclear how much this mindless male role behavior contributed to the demise of his first marriage, but Tracy experienced it as the main cause of their marital difficulties. She recalled what was for her a deeply significant moment which had caused her pain and anguish but had also freed her from delusionary expectations of Brad.

They were at a party and she saw him pour some of his drink into a glass and push it across the table to a woman with whom he worked. It was an intimate gesture, which he had done many times with Tracy, who had seen it as a special, endearing exchange. When she saw him repeat the behavior in what appeared to be exactly the same way, she realized she had been deluding herself. The delusion involved a sense of romance and security. She had her man, her Prince Charming, who would always see her as beautiful, always want to touch her and make love to her, and to whom no other woman would be as important. That incident shattered the delusion.

Thereafter, Tracy saw Brad as insincere, superficial, and eventually, undesirable as a mate. Brad was amazed and angry that she reacted in that way: "She has always been possessive. All I have to do is look at another woman and she notices." Brad was right. Tracy, like most women, had been conditioned to expect single minded devotion from her man, according to the romantic ideal. If she didn't receive single-minded devotion, it meant Brad didn't love her. Brainwashed by the words of the popular song, "I Only Have Eyes for You." That meant that if Brad loved her, he wouldn't notice other women, let alone actively pay attention to them. Her expectation was that he would continue to treat her as if she were special--and so the delusion continued, until too many real-world incidents had accumulated and it was no longer possible for her to see Brad as the man of her dreams.

Brad noticed how Tracy, like his first wife, changed from a loving, smiling woman to a distant, cold, and suspicious one. He mourned the transformation, never realizing the extent to which he himself had changed: "She knew what she was getting. I never pretended to be anything other than myself, which is more than I can say for her. When we started to date, she loved oral sex. She was the sexiest woman I ever met. That lasted about a year. Then she started complaining that I didn't shower before I came to bed. Or I didn't kiss her enough. Hell, most guys don't want to go through all that red tape just to get a blow job." In Brad's mind, the "red tape" conflicted with the ideal of being sexually serviced because the woman desperately needs and loves you.

As Brad talked about his disappointment in Tracy, he began to listen to himself and to slowly realize that his behaviors had contributed to Tracy's sexual disinterest. It sobered him. He felt remorse, he wanted to make it right. But it was not to be with Tracy. She had found another Prince Charming, another man of her dreams. She started the delusionary cycle all over again, replacing Brad with a younger, more attentive version of the male stereotype. Without insight into her delusions and unrealistic expectations, Tracy was doomed to repeat the cycle over and over again.

It seemed tragic that Tracy had never gotten to know Brad as a real person. She had fallen in love with a stereotype, and her positive feelings had subsided and dissipated when Brad emerged as just a confused man. Brad was confused. He didn't know how to make it work. He felt like a failure--and Tracy didn't talk to him about it. She just withdrew and nursed her hurt and resentment.

Brad was amazed that Tracy left him, found another man, and never looked back. He thought she had needed him, loved him, and would always be in his power. However, his sense of entitlement, like that of most men, was over-blown. His culture, through the example his father and brothers had set for him, taught him that women were less than men, weaker, and therefore, dependent on men for their protection and livelihood. Brad's expectation was that Tracy would always be there, supportive and understanding, even if he neglected her. This view of male-female relationships was reinforced by all aspects of the media, but in reality, Tracy, like his first wife, was not powerless. She was educated, competent, and totally capable of taking care of herself. But Tracy had also been affected by gender-based messages that shaped her into a rough approximation of the female stereotype. Like Brad, she thought she needed him.

When she first met him, he appeared to be the perfect image of the ideal man. He courted her, was very generous and attentive, and finally won her. After the marriage, one of the single most important factors contributing to his attraction to her disappeared. The chase was over, the prize had been won. She was his, or so he thought. Brad was very aroused by the chase, the challenge of pursuit, and the victory, but now he had scored and the game was over, just like in school. But now, however, they were married and committed and Tracy expected the fairy tale to continue. So did Brad, but it didn't happen that way. Brad stopped courting and Tracy stopped caring.

The culture had deluded them. Educational forces in the culture had not conditioned Brad and Tracy to be attracted and interested in each other after the chase and commitment had occurred. They were left with failed expectations. They felt duped: marriage and commitment felt like a bait and switch. Promised much, given little. The natural result was anger and self doubt. Both Brad and Tracy had followed the gender-based injunctions for naught. What was to be done? Repeat the cycle with someone else? Maintain the relationship with renewed determination to force oneself and mate into cookie cutter images of the stereotype? Rail at the culture and circumstances that had produced this delusionary system? Withdraw and give up relating to anyone since it was so very difficult and resulted in so little satisfaction and happiness? All of these options have been tested by others with similar problems. None has proven successful. The solution is more complex. It involves an educational process that starts in the primary grades and continues through secondary education and college. This type of material must be integrated into our general education curriculum.

Victory or Defeat

Chapter 7

The Functional Basis of Stereotypes

A child is alone in the middle of a dense forest. The trees are tall and their foliage obscures the sunlight. It is hard to see. The child looks around for a way out. There are no clear markers. The child feels lost and afraid. Looking down, the child sees what appears to be a path. Hope stirs within. Someone has passed this way before and found a way out! The child scans the forest floor for other markings. Not knowing exactly where the path will lead, but it is still better than no path at all. The child wants to follow another's footprints rather than striking out independently. Coming to a clearing, the child sees other children, all wearing the same garments. There is a similar garment on the ground that will fit. The child puts on the garment and joins the group, blending in perfectly. Is this victory or defeat?

Conformity offers comfort and security. To minimize disorder and confusion, we establish some general guidelines for behaviors and beliefs: we construct stereotypes. We do this to support our common interests and characteristics. Those of us who follow the guidelines and accept the stereotypes develop a certain sameness, a collective identity that sometimes obliterates our individuality and forces us into conventions that typify our group. Since this goes on for generations, we are usually unaware of this process and its impact on our lives. In fact, we embrace the customs and repetitiveness that structures our lives and resent those who do not adhere to our belief system. If they become too disruptive, we cast them out in order to protect our belief system and our community. We teach our young the rules by modeling and assigning position and social status based on conformity. Gender, economics, and other considerations are interwoven with an elaborate system of rewards and punishments. This process is designed to insure orderly, sequential steps in our development. The system prevents us from becoming fearful of life's various stages. We know what to expect and what is expected of us. When we are uncertain, we utilize these guidelines and stereotypes to fix ourselves firmly--sometimes too much so--in place. This can have either positive or negative consequences.

Positive valuing of the conventional stereotypes resulted in success and happiness for Stan. Born on the wrong side of the tracks to a poor, uneducated family, Stan had little or no access to the middle class community. He did not know how to act, dress, or talk to gain acceptance to the economic and social class to which he aspired. His parents and siblings seemed to be steeped in lower class values and behaviors. In order to overcome them, Stan had to tutor himself. He liked to read books and watch television shows that typified middle- or upper-class characters and families. He tried to emulate what he saw upper-middle-class people do. He rejected his own family. Not angrily or rebelliously, but with an overwhelming feeling of shame. He was ashamed of their poverty and lack of education.

When he was in jr high he got a job as a bag boy in a suburban grocery store. It was far from his home but worth the long walk across town because he had an opportunity to see firsthand how successful people dressed, spoke, and lived. He developed the habit of buying his clothes in a thrift shop: it was the only way he could dress stylishly. He was careful to select clothing similar to that worn by the boys he wanted to be like. He worked hard at school to improve his grammar and flinched whenever he heard anyone in his family say "ain't" or use any poor grammar.

He was bright, so he was able to earn a scholarship to a small liberal arts college, where he majored in political science. He was extremely appreciative of the opportunity. He couldn't understand how some of his fellow students cut class and blew off cultural events the college offered to enrich student life. Stan treasured every moment of every class as an opportunity to better himself, and it worked for him. His grade average was always high. He paid particular attention to social skills. He learned to dance, to make small talk, and to flirt, all by observing and mimicking the behavior and mannerisms of his chosen middle class models. He was pleasant and gracious and never missed an opportunity to make a social contact or present himself in a favorable manner. Soon after graduation, he successfully ran for political office in county government. In three years he had saved enough money to go to law school. He was anxious, so much so, that he was overcome with test anxiety and had to take the LSAT (Law School Admission Test) twice before he was admitted to law school at the state university. Stan was afraid he wouldn't make it even if he followed the rules, but he was very persistent. His goals were clear.

The stereotypes and guidelines functioned well for Stan. He made many friends who respected his diligence and persistence. Stan realized the American dream. He did so by complying with the guidelines and believing in the system. He made himself part of it. Stan played by the rules until he was a respected member of the community. He married a nice girl from a good family, had a daughter, and went on to become a leader in his community. He could not have done so without clarifying and studying the conventions and guidelines set out for group behavior. Stan did not feel like a conformist or an opportunist--he felt blessed. He had achieved what he wanted. It didn't matter that he was an ordinary, middle-class guy. That's all he ever wanted. To fit in. To be upwardly mobile.

Ironically, many people who have the kind of life Stan worked so hard to achieve do not appreciate it. They devalue it, and find the customs and conventions trite and hackneyed. They are bored and unappreciative of their lives and take their status in the community for granted. Moreover, many of their children openly defy the traditions and customs. They hold the conventional stereotypes in contempt, preferring to become part of a subculture. Stereotypes do not function as successfully when there is little perceived need to succeed.

Stan's daughter, Carrie, was very different from her father at age seventeen. Instead of respecting convention and utilizing it, as her father had done, to make her position in society more secure, she devalued it and played at being a nonconformist. Perhaps she knew she could do so because her father was secure enough in his position to rescue her if need be.

Her nonconformity was dramatic. She pierced her nose and wore a red sequined nose ring in it. Her makeup was flamboyant and she dressed in a deliberately provocative manner. Poor taste. A badge of defiance, but it was also an effective statement of her feelings. Carrie didn't need to follow rules or develop herself. Her father's success made that superfluous.

Stan brought her to my office. He was beside himself with anxiety. She was glad to come. It was cool to have a "shrink." She had no goals in counseling; she just wanted someone to talk to. I soon realized that underneath her bravado she felt lost and unwanted. Her parents were distant. They were private people, preoccupied with their own interests and unwilling to share their feelings with their daughter or anyone else. Her parents hoped her conversations with me would stabilize her and limit her acting out behavior. They did not seek a closer relationship with their daughter. What they wanted was to control her behavior, to force her adherence to cultural guidelines.

I recommended family sessions rather than individual ones. Change would not occur without involving the total system.

Our sessions focused on interchanges between Carrie and her parents. They expressed their negative feelings about her debunking their values. That didn't get anywhere; it bored Carrie, she had heard it before. However, something magical happened when Stan began to talk about himself. Carrie listened intently to her father's descriptions of his early life and how he had developed his cherished values. She felt flattered and honored that he had stepped out of the role of successful community leader for her sake. More importantly, she felt that she was getting to know him for the first time as a person, and not just a father. The experience seemed to transform her. "I've always seen him as a fat cat. He never even hinted that his family was poor. It's cool the way he made it on his own." Her eyes misted.

Carrie's mother, Sarah, was an attractive woman who didn't say much. She faded into the background while Stan and Carrie talked about their relationship. Sarah was disturbed that Stan had concealed so much from her. Like Carrie, she was amazed when she learned about Stan's childhood. Toward the end of one of our family sessions she broke her silence. Addressing her husband with anger, "You married me for the wrong reason. I'm just a piece in your puzzle, someone to perfect your image. We've been married almost twenty years and I don't even know you. You've never told me any of this." She was dry eyed and spoke softly, but her body was tense. She was very upset. "You used me. You tricked me. You've never loved me."

Stan was clearly shaken by his wife's accusation. "It's not that way now. I've always loved you. And now I love you more than anything in my life."

Sarah didn't believe him and restated her reaction: "The only reason you've leveled with us is because of Carrie. I have nothing to do with it. I feel degraded." Silence. The session was over. Carrie had never seen so much emotion flow between her parents. She was fascinated by the interchange. It was the most significant interchange she had ever witnessed between her parents. It seemed to bond her to them. For the first time in my presence, she touched them both.

They filed out of my office grimly. I knew they would talk about it on their own. They did. Stan and Sarah reached an understanding about how their relationship had begun. Sarah was right. She had attracted Stan because of what she symbolized. She had never realized that before. It hurt her, but she felt better when she expressed her anger and Stan acknowledged that her status had been part of his initial attraction to her.

Sharing his feelings was very difficult for Stan. He believed that his success rested on his ability to build an image that concealed his poverty. He had truly felt he wasn't good enough for Sarah when they first met and married. For him, it was a miracle of sorts that he had realized his dream. He kept his contacts with his family of origin to a minimum. In fact, they were not even represented at the wedding. They were part of a past he had chosen to leave behind, but now he had to speak the truth to save Carrie and hold on to Sarah. Feelings of shame swept over him. He made no effort to hide. He was more powerful in his honesty than ever before.

Sarah and Carrie were incredulous that he felt shame instead of pride. They respected him but felt sad that he had been so secretive. Stan told Sarah several times that he did love her but felt unworthy to be her mate.

I'm not certain she truly accepted his reassurance, or believed that he really loved her, but their relationship was certainly strengthened as a result of this confrontation with reality. They had built a good life together and wanted to maintain it and help their daughter establish herself. To do that they had to humanize their relationship by increasing intimacy and sharing truth.

Carrie was touched by her mother's emotion. Throughout her childhood, she had never seen her mother cry or show much depth of feeling. She had concluded that her mother was cold and unemotional. Carrie, in turn, concealed her own feelings, modeling herself after her mother. She was very disappointed in herself when she realized that she also appeared cold and unfeeling. Part of what she was trying to do when she broke away from family values was to express her feelings. She was relieved and excited when she witnessed the conflict between her parents. It gave her hope for herself. Maybe she wouldn't have to behave so outrageously to prove she had feelings. Confrontation with the truth seemed to liberate them all.

Carrie did stabilize and actually affirmed her father's value system. I believe the change occurred because she learned more about him as a person and how he had lived when he was her age. When he spoke of the poverty and his shame at being so ignorant and poor, it brought tears to her eyes. Since he had never told her or her mother about this aspect of his background, it seemed more dramatic when he did. This often is the case with family secrets. They become overcharged with emotion. The emotion dissipates once a secret is shared.

Stan was ashamed. He wanted to forget, but as he talked to his daughter of his fear that she would revert to the life that he had struggled so hard to escape, she was touched by his passion and began to see the value of what he had accomplished. She felt motivated to set some goals for herself. "It's not the money," she said, "but the process that I respect. He knew how to hang tight. I have to learn that."

Carrie did learn to "hang tight." She accepted her father as a model and reembraced the values he stood for, but not in the same way that he did. She was cockier and much more of a risk taker, but she applied herself more diligently in school and became a leader in her own way. The system worked for her as it had for her father. She developed her own brand of community spirit. Carrie accepted the functional value of the conventional stereotype only after it had been humanized for her. This could not have happened without insight into her father's development. Her father educated her by sharing his personal experience in depth. Without this it is unlikely that she would have seen the value in the cultural guidelines he had followed. It was a painful experience for both of them--for Stan, the father, because he had wanted to keep his past a secret and he had to revisit his pain in order to share his past, and for Carrie because she saw her father's pain and was moved by it.

It is unclear whether Carrie's affirmation of family values would have occurred without the counseling experience. Family ties were strengthened as a result of our sessions, but this could have occurred without Carrie's affirmation of her father's values. Intergenerationally, there is an inclination toward positive acceptance of family values when affection and warmth exists in the family of origin. Oftentimes children reject their parents because they feel they have been treated unjustly. Parental values are then likewise rejected. The values are unacceptable to the child because of their association with the rejected parental figures. It is a process of overgeneralization. Carrie may have reaffirmed her father's value system as a result of her increased respect and acceptance of him as a person.

The affirmation of values passed on by pervious generations becomes more complex when sexual orientation is a factor.

Kathy was lesbian. She had three brothers and had always felt that she, too, should have been a boy. Her family was poor. They lived in a small three bedroom house. Her brothers resented the fact that she was given her own room while they had to share their space with two other siblings. Girl's clothes were also more expensive than boys. They had to share. Wearing hand-me-downs was something they hated. Kathy's clothes were always new. When her brothers weren't teasing her, they ignored her. She hated being a girl.

Kathy's mother, Janell, enjoyed having a daughter and lavished attention on her. Janell always wanted Kathy by her side when she gardened. She also taught her to sew and bake, accomplishments in which Janell and her sisters excelled. The expectation was that Kathy would enjoy homemaking and be a mother. The family also had a tradition of leadership in 4-H. Kathy was expected to carry on that tradition. Kathy had no interest in these activities. She longed for playmates who would accept her.

By the time she was eleven, Kathy knew she was different from other girls. It wasn't until tenth grade that she learned enough about homosexuality to identify herself as lesbian. Her greatest desire was to get away from home so she could find others like herself. She felt very alone. There was no one she could talk to about her identity. She loved her mother deeply and was heartsick at the prospect of telling her that she could not fulfill her expectations. She did not want to be a mother or a homemaker. She didn't know what she wanted to be, only that she wanted to get away.

She joined the army immediately after graduation from high school. It was not long before she formed a relationship with another woman. Kathy was happier than she had ever been. She was free to be herself. Although homosexuality was not openly accepted in the Armed Forces, it was easy to maintain clandestine, same sex-relationships. Kathy enjoyed living with women and focusing on her own development.

Her relationship with her family was strained. She kept her sexual identity a secret. Janell, her mother, was devastated when Kathy joined the army. She took it as a personal rejection of her own values. She felt like a failure. She had not raised a daughter she could be proud of. Whenever anyone asked about Kathy, Janell felt embarrassed. The daughters of her sisters and friends were having babies. Her daughter was in the army, stationed in a distant part of the country. Janell longed for a daughter she could see regularly. She also wanted to pass along her wisdom on homemaking and parenting. But this was not to be. Janell had to accept it. There was nothing else she could do. Her heart ached.

When Kathy came home on leave and brought a girlfriend, Janell had a strange feeling that something was really amiss, but she was afraid to ask. Kathy's father, Ralph, thought nothing of it, or at least he didn't say anything. So Janell remained silent. Kathy said nothing about her sexual issue. They just behaved normally until it felt normal. Gradually, the family grew accustomed to Kathy's friend, Bernice. At Christmas, Bernice and Kathy spent some time with each of their respective families. Everything went along smoothly until Kathy and Bernice broke up. Kathy was very upset and wanted maternal comforting, so she called her mother and told her about her sexual identity and the breakup. Janell was not totally surprised that Kathy was lesbian. She was able to be minimally supportive. However, she was deeply disappointed, she felt she had let her daughter down. Soon afterward, Janell developed a depression. Her minister referred her to me for consultation. Janell said: "I know I ought to be able to handle this, and I will, but right now all I can think about is everything I'm going to miss. I'll never be able to talk to my friends about her or show off her children." The fact that her sons could reproduce and make her a grandmother did not compensate for her loss. "When your daughter marries, you gain a son. When your son marries, you lose a son." She sounded confused, but the words were unimportant. She was grieving.

She had come to my office alone. Unable to share her feelings with her husband or anyone else. Except for me, a therapist. whom she would never see again. It was a long session. When she had scheduled it she had asked for a double session. She talked and cried freely, it was a strange experience.

I see many clients for only one session, particularly about sexual concerns. Janell, like many others, wanted to talk about her daughter's sexual identity with someone who would understand. It made her comfortable to think that I knew about lesbians and accepted them. "I've read your book," she said. "My minister loaned it to me." I nodded, not knowing for sure which part of my book she thought applied to her daughter, Kathy.

When Janell's time was up, she paid me in cash and left. She had accepted Kathy's identity and expressed her fear that her daughter would have a hard life. Janell grieved the loss of shared traditions. She found solace in continuing to love her daughter regardless of the differences in their respective value systems.

I was aware that much of this unhappiness could have been avoided with preventative education by providing acceptable alternative stereotypes that could function successfully for the nonheterosexual segment of the population. Families with homosexual members need acknowledgment and support, which the current educational system fails to provide.

Ideally, affirmation of values occurs at both a cognitive and affective level. Our culture does not provide an orderly process whereby this can be accomplished.

Our procedures for punishing or expelling disruptive persons who do not follow the guidelines or embrace communal stereotypes are sometimes inconsistent and selectively enforced. Guidelines involving national security are more rigidly enforced. The military stereotype cannot be evaded or even discounted without invoking strong reactions.

Just prior to the Persian Gulf War, Martin served in the U.S. Army Reserves. He received monthly checks for functioning as an officer in the reserve forces during peacetime. When it came time to report for active duty, he declared his unwillingness to go based on conscientious objection to the war which he saw as a result of political opportunism of the party in power.

His father was mortified and his entire family exerted pressure on Martin to do his duty and fulfill his military obligation. His girlfriend did not want him to go but urged him to comply on the basis of her own family's reaction to his refusal. They saw it as cowardice. The pressure was enormous.

Martin gave in and went. He fulfilled his duty, came home safely, but had great difficulty forgiving himself for "copping out," as he called it. He felt he had betrayed his own value system: "I should have stood my ground. Everybody remembers that I didn't want to go but was forced to. I lost all the way around."

When I asked him to explore the process he had gone through, he admitted to being confused. "I didn't know whether I was being selfish or courageous by not complying. In the end, I was temporarily convinced that I should do it for the greater good. I still don't know if I did the right thing. What I do know is that I lost the respect of my family and friends for standing my ground and objecting--and then, when I gave in, they respected me even less. I couldn't win. I guess I'm not supposed to think for myself."

Martin was experiencing the consequences of straying from the beaten path. He could not understand why he could not engage in dissent without encountering so much pressure. "No one even asked me why I didn't want to go. They just assumed the worst: that I was a coward or a cheat. But that's not true. Ever since Vietnam, it's been okay to question what the government wants to do in wartime. This is a democracy. It's supposed to be okay to think for yourself!" His eyes were blazing. His words came out with a bellow of defiance.

I was struck by his naivete. It was strangely beautiful, and incredibly sad. Martin was speaking the truth as he knew it. He had acted on his beliefs, which he actually thought were in line with messages he had received from trusted mentors in his life. He felt misunderstood and betrayed. Everyone had turned against him. Even worse, he had turned against himself.

The final blow came when his girlfriend, Delores, broke up with him, saying: "I can't wait around for you to grow up. Toughen up. The world is not a playground. Just get on with your life. Everyone's going to forget about it. The war is over."

The war was not over for Martin--it raged within. He had seen things he would never forget. Before the war, he had not known how vicious men could be--how they could kill and mutilate. He did not want to be part of it. It wasn't right to be part of it. He needed reassurance that he wasn't crazy for thinking the way he did. Everyone else was pretending that war was just that way and nothing could be done about it. Martin thought he had a responsibility to resist something he knew wasn't right.

Martin had bad dreams. Some nights he was afraid to go to bed and close his eyes. He kept seeing the mutilated bodies of women and children nailed to posts outside Kuwait. It was horrible--medieval. He had not known people still did things like that. It sickened him. It disillusioned him.

He had tried to talk to Delores about it, but she didn't want to hear it. She was the kind of person that couldn't go to horror movies, so she couldn't begin to listen to Martin describe the atrocities he had witnessed. Alienation resulted because Martin couldn't share the way he felt with her. He distanced himself emotionally until finally they rarely spoke except for superficial comments about external things like the weather. They didn't enjoy touching anymore.

Delores came in to see me before she broke up with Martin. "He's a completely different person. He used to be so sensitive. He hasn't told me he loved me for months. One of the things I liked about him was his ability to talk about his feelings and be affectionate."

I interjected, "You seem to feel this is a permanent change." She started to cry. "Yes, he'll never be the same. I'll never see him the same way again. My family doesn't respect him because he tried to evade his military duty." "What about you? How did that affect your feelings?" I asked.

She sighed and remained silent for several minutes. "It's like I grew up overnight and saw the whole world differently. My oldest brother was killed in Vietnam. He didn't want to go either. I never dreamed Martin was like that. I guess I didn't know him. I should have ended it right then, but it seemed so disloyal. I thought I might change my mind when he did go. But after he came back, he was so different; and he can't stop talking about it. It's all he thinks about. He's so messed up--no fun to be with. I tried to snap him out of it, but it didn't work. I hope you can help him."

Martin was unprepared for the end of the relationship. His grief about losing Delores compounded his reaction to his traumatic military experience. That added to his confusion. Martin had lived with confusion all his life.

As I listened to him, it became clear that he had been unable to organize and integrate the conflicting messages he had received throughout his life about right and wrong. He had always noted the inconsistencies in what he was taught. Even when he was a small child he had noticed how his parents did things they told him not to do. It confused him. Although he had successfully completed school and held a job, including one in the armed forces, he had not thoroughly synthesized the conglomeration of rules, regulations, guidelines, ideals, and beliefs with which he had been deluged.

Martin had an above-average IQ and his score on the Minnesota Multiphasic Personality Inventory (MMPI) indicated no pathology. He had no underlying mental disorder--he simply disagreed with the group norms. Serious consequences followed. He was forced to do something he did not believe in. He was punished for expressing his feelings. He knew laws had to be followed or there would be chaos: Martin had thought he understood. He thought there was room for dissent and nonconformity within the group. He had been told that was the case in a democracy. But the rules for dissenting were so complex that it made dissent difficult, if not impossible.   Martin explored the development of his confusion. He had grown accustomed to cognitive dissonance as a child and young adult. He had never received satisfactory explanations when he asked for clarification. He remembered his father giving him condoms when he was fourteen. This occurred after both his parents had told him to wait to have sex until he was married or in a committed relationship. Martin was horrified and embarrassed when his father gave him the condoms and asked what he was supposed to do with them if he was not allowed to have sex. His father said: "I just don't want you to get into trouble. I know kids don't always follow the rules." Martin felt very sad because he sensed his father didn't trust him. After that he had trouble trusting his father, or the rules.

Normal incidents like this one, which many people can absorb without difficulty, disturbed Martin. He needed more information than he was given to help him understand the pluralism inherent in life's decisions. There were many double messages and no one taught him how to sort them out.

The rejection he experienced from his parents and girlfriend both hurt and embittered him. Martin felt abandoned in time of need. Prior to this experience,

Martin felt the world was a friendly place. He enjoyed life. Despite the cognitive dissonance, he was able to function successfully. He had felt secure in his place in his family and the community. His life circumstance was altered considerably by his forced participation in the Persian Gulf War. It came at a time when developmentally Martin was consolidating his identity as an adult male. His condition would be classified In The Diagnostic and Statistical Manual of Mental Disorders as V62.89 "Phase of Life Problem or Other Life Circumstance." This is not considered a mental disorder--at least health insurance providers refuse to cover it. Martin was unprepared for the stressors he encountered. He was mildly handicapped by his sensitivity and idealism. He tried to behave honorably, based on a confused belief system.

I have known many Martins--people who have difficulty adjusting to cultural expectations because they do not quite understand them. I often ponder my own responsibility in complying with and supporting a social and educational structure than can be so damaging to the very people it is trying to educate and protect.

Martin recovered and got on with his life, but he held on to his anger. He thought the situation was un fair. *What do you think? Should individual fairness be an issue; or is the greater good always on the side of the majority?*

Martin yielded to group pressure, sacrificing his individuality to support the interests of the larger community. Perhaps this is appropriate, but there is little doubt that Martin was not prepared for the pressure he experienced. The educational system failed him and subsequently punished him for its own failure.

Others in his predicament assimilated the cultural messages and conformed with less dissonance and pain. Martin felt like a victim. Our culture is impatient with victims, tending to focus on their responsibility to help themselves and avoid punishment.

Cultural responsibility is clearly a factor.

Had Martin's family and girlfriend been more open to the concept of dissent and the process of engaging in it, Martin might have received more understanding and support for his position. His parents were unable to acknowledge his true identity because they were focused on the stereotype of the young male going off to war to protect hearth and home. Delores, his girlfriend, was unable to accept his behavior because it seemed unmanly and contradicted the values in her family of origin. Martin did not fit the stereotype for what a male was supposed to be which rendered him undesirable as a mate.

Should the stereotype be adjusted to fit Martin or should Martin be forced into the stereotype?   Perhaps Martin would have complied more readily if his cognitive dissonance had been diagnosed and treated earlier in his development.

The functional value of stereotypes must be acknowledged. Problems arise when an individual is unaware of the stereotype he or she is attempting to approximate or when the guidelines for behavior are perceived to be rigid and unbending. Healthy adherence to stereotypes and group norms need not obliterate individuality and spontaneity. It is essential to have a conscious awareness of the guiding stereotype to accomplish a working fit. The most extreme problems result from situations in which thoughts and behaviors are controlled only by simplistic preconscious beliefs, such as "Patriotism is good" or "War is bad."

We have explored cases in which unconscious forces controlled the selection of friends or mates. Attraction is based as much on unconscious and preconscious factors as it is on conscious ones. Sexual arousal is frequently dependent on a shadowy stereotype which is cued as a result of subliminal association. Sexual arousal is linked with cultural ideals or stereotypes. If a female has been conditioned to associate sexual arousal with male dominance and youth and selects a mate who possesses those qualities, initially she will be sexually aroused by him. If they marry or live together, over time the female will see her mate in enough nondominant situations that the association with arousal will fade. As her mate ages, the arousal link with youth may further inhibit her sexual response to her now middle-aged mate. The stereotype linking youth and dominance with sexual arousal will be initially successful in bonding the two people sexually. As time goes on, however, the stereotype will have the opposite effect. The arousal association will no longer operate because the male is no longer seen as dominant and young. The initial linking remains, but the people no longer fit the stereotype. Thus, disorders of sexual arousal are inherent in our current male stereotypes of youthful dominance. The reverse is also true. If males are conditioned to respond only to young females, their arousal response will wane if they are mated with a middle-aged female. Surely we can do better than this in the preparation of our young. To make the stereotype more functional and expand its original purpose of attraction and reproduction, a couple must be able to overcome the impact of a fading stereotype before it becomes destructive and dissipates sexual attraction and arousal.

Suzanne and Ted were very attracted to one other when they first met. She was thirty-two and he was thirty-four. They both looked young for their age. Both had been married previously and been divorced for over six years when they first met. The "chemistry" was great--they felt as if they were "in heat." There was also a great deal of romance in their interactions. Ted came on strong. He played the part of being a male; acted decisive, more so than he really felt. He was playing a part. He also did small repair jobs around Suzanne's house fulfilling another male stereotype which generated the predicted response in Suzanne: she enjoyed having him around and feeling like she had a male in her life again. Sex was good, they laughed a lot. It was fun. They felt young, as if they had been given another chance at life. Both had felt a bit like a failure when the first marriage ended in divorce.

Suzanne and Ted moved in together. After about eighteen months, however, their relationship began to change. Ted started cooking dinner because Suzanne worked later than he did and he also started doing some of the housework. Suzanne appreciated this because she was too tired to do it all herself. Gradually, her arousal response to Ted diminished. She said it was because he looked older, had gained some weight, and also sometimes looked rather dumpy when he was cooking or cleaning. Her perception of him had changed. She now associated him with comfort, security, and home--but not sexual arousal. For Suzanne, that was still linked to youth and dominance. The stereotype was no longer functional. Ted was no longer young and Suzanne did not want to be dominated in her marriage. The early associations of youth and sex, which had been functional in junior high and high school and throughout the dating period, were now forming the basis of a sexual dysfunction.

Ted felt undesirable. Suzanne no longer responded with arousal when he put his arms around her. She just smiled affectionately and went to sleep. When they talked about the problem, she tried to make suggestions for different kinds of touch that might be more arousing. The message was that there was something wrong with approach to lovemaking. Ted lost confidence in himself and began having trouble with his erections. Then he, too, began to avoid sex. By the time the couple arrived at my office they were both extremely unhappy with what had once been a highly romanticized sexual relationship.

We talked about their feelings and they both stated they wanted to revive their old "in heat" feelings. They asked me if that was possible. They had already tried to revive the old feelings by playing out their first date, but that just didn't work anymore. They had to build new associations with sensuality and eroticism. It wasn't difficult, but it required work and they both resented that they had to work at something that was supposed to be fun. They started taking baths together, giving each other oil rubs, and having dinner in front of the fireplace. They reestablished candlelight during their sexual encounters. The underlying feeling was nuturance rather than eroticized romance. It was effective, but the real magic started when they let go of their inhibitions and became more intimate during their sexual encounters. They stimulated themselves in the presence of one another, maintained eye contact during orgasm, and told each other their innermost fantasies. It made a difference. They felt like they were exploring their sexuality together at a deeper level than before. It was a fresh experience. Their sexual encounters were exciting because each took responsibility for initiation and fulfillment.

This differed markedly from the gender-based sexual encounters that characterized their early romance. Ted was no longer solely responsible for giving Suzanne an orgasm. Suzanne started taking more control over the positions they used during sex. She refused to have sex with Ted unless he had bathed and shaved. They departed from the previous role-bound guidelines that had defined their sexual relationship. What they accomplished was developmentally sound: a new sexual relationship based on commitment, nuturance, and openness. They had successfully outgrown the stereotype and replaced it with a more genuine intimacy.

Attraction and reproduction are not adequate binders in a marriage. They serve a primary function, which ideally gives way to more enduring motivators. This process would be more functional if it were made clear to all learners in primary and secondary grades so that realistic relationship formation could become as familiar as the multiplication tables and the ABCs.

Family Mural

Chapter 8

Realistic Relationship Formation

Imagine that you have been married for many years to someone who has concealed their true identity from you. Someone who pretended to be heterosexual, as you are, but is not. Someone who feigned arousal during sexual encounters and played the romantic role so well that you never even suspected you had married a homosexual. Your entire relationship is founded on deceit and delusion.

This is what happened to David. What disturbed him the most was that his wife, Margaret, did not ever choose to be honest. One of David's clients, a woman whose home and office he had designed and decorated, told him. His client was lesbian and knew that Margaret was gay and had frequented gay bars for years. It was common knowledge in the local lesbian community that Margaret had at least two serious relationships with women during the time she had been married to David.

He was stunned by her duplicitous behavior. She did not deny it when he confronted her, nor did she apologize. That was not her style. She expected him to accept it and live with it for the sake of their adopted child, Leslie. Margaret was very angry with David's client for betraying the unwritten subcultural code that you never blow some-one's cover. She refused to acknowledge any wrongdoing on her own part.

David consulted me because he could not make up his mind whether to sue Margaret for fraud or just divorce her. "Realistically," he said, "I will never trust her again. She deceived me and would have continued doing so if my client hadn't informed me." He buried his face in his hands, "I can't believe I was so stupid!" He felt shame. To be betrayed was bad enough, but to have others know his wife was unfaithful when he did not made it worse, much worse. He spent several weeks expressing what felt to him like unbearable shame before he could start to consider his options.

Divorce was an obvious option. He had been duped: Margaret had lied to him over and over again. He now thought everything he had believed to be true about their relationship was a lie. He couldn't understand why Margaret didn't want a divorce so she could be free to relate openly to her women friends. He concluded that she had never loved him; just used him for a cover. Margaret did not deny this. But she wanted to stay married.

"I don't want to be part of a subculture," she said, "I like being in the closet. I love David. We have a good life together. We both love Leslie. Now that he knows, it can be even better. I won't have to hide from him. If he really loves me, he will understand."

She sounded brittle and uncaring, oblivious to the pain her deception had caused David. She expressed no remorse, perhaps because she herself was so used to pain. Hardened by the difficulties of being lesbian in a world that labeled her sexual preference deviant and forced her to pretend to be something she was not, Margaret hadn't developed the same moral code or sense of empathy she might have if the mainstream culture had accepted her sexual identity. She had always felt different and had always concealed it. That did something to her inside: it made her less likely to uphold values that supported the mainstream community, which oppressed her. No wonder she was callous to David's reaction. Her lesbian feelings had never been considered a viable issue. She had no first-hand experience with empathy as no one had sympathized with her plight. I tried to teach her compassion in our sessions by empathizing with her. I felt very supportive of her. She had experienced a great deal of anguish in her life. I could see it in her eyes when she described how her family and friends made disparaging remarks about gays, not knowing her secret. She was afraid to come out of the closet for fear she would be attacked and have everything she had earned taken from her.

She spoke of how painful it was to have her feelings denied. When she finally told her father, he said she was too young to know what she really felt or wanted and that choosing a lesbian life would be a mistake. Something that would hurt others and she could never take back. Margaret heeded her father's remarks and remained closeted. How did that affect her? Denying her own feelings had made it easy to discount the feelings of others, as with David, her husband. "Why should his feelings be more important than mine?" she reasoned.

"If I can betray myself, I can betray anyone. Besides, I never lied to him. I never told him I wasn't lesbian. It just never came up."

David was sickened by her rationalizations. She was not the woman he thought he had married. He decided to sue for divorce and for custody of Leslie. Margaret was terrified at the prospect of being exposed, which would happen if they went through court proceedings. She would also lose her daughter, Leslie, whom she loved very much. David said he wouldn't bring up her sexual identity if she would forgo a financial settlement and visitation rights with their child. He wanted to punish her.

What felt like a harsh position, bordering on blackmail, to Margaret seemed very justifiable to David. "She really isn't fit to be a mother, not because she's lesbian, but because she's a lying sneak. She doesn't deserve anything I've worked for since she was cheating on me from the very beginning. I was just too stupid to see it. She's turned her last trick on me."

Margaret pleaded with him to reconsider. I could see him wavering, but the most he would agree to was a four-month waiting period during which they met weekly in my office to resolve their feelings. "The only reason I'm agreeing to this," he said, "is that I'm afraid she'll kill herself, and I don't want her blood on my hands." He was rationalizing. Margaret had never threatened suicide, but her crying and sobbing softened David's heart. Thus began four months of the most intense relationship reformation I have ever witnessed.

It was important for David to get to know Margaret as she really was. He did not want to be lied to or fooled anymore. Their entire relationship had been based on subterfuge: it had clearly been delusionary. He had made many assumptions about her based on his own perceptions and belief system. Since he would never have tricked someone the way she had tricked him, it never occurred to him that it could happen. He had assumed her values were similar to his own, a common error in delusional relationship formation. During the ensuing sessions, he insisted on knowing everything about her feelings, even if it caused him great pain. He asked her how she felt when they were having sex. Was it repugnant to her? Had all her sighs and moans been fake? Did she laugh at him behind his back and joke about him with her female lovers? These were agonizing questions. His face whitened and his eyes teared as he rasped out his inquiries.

At first Margaret couldn't respond. His emotion overwhelmed her. She had never seen this side of him before. She realized he had feelings, just as women did. A simple discovery, but it made a difference in her perception of him and her ability to trust and love him. So she told him her true feelings about him and the sexual experiences they had shared. There were a few times when it had been really good, but for the most part she found penetration painful since she was slow to lubricate and he focused on his own pleasure rather than her discomfort. "Why didn't you tell me?" His reaction to her lack of assertiveness was outrage. How was he supposed to know what made her feel good? "Just because I'm a man doesn't mean I sprang from the womb with a leap of sexual prowess, knowing all about sex. You think you are so liberated--why can't you communicate with me? Stop trying to typecast me. Do you expect your women lovers to know what to do without telling them anything? I don't think so!"

Margaret acknowledged that she had unrealistic expectations of David. She had picked up the idea somewhere that men were supposed to lead the way in sex. She acted in accordance with that belief when she was sexual with David, although it ran counter to her natural inclination. That is one of the reasons why she preferred to relate to women. There was more equality in sex--as in every-thing else. Also, her women lovers had a softer touch and didn't need so much instruction regarding when and where to touch her. Since Margaret had picked up the idea that men could not handle feedback about their lovemaking, she usually allowed David to use her body rather than actively participate in sexual encounters. She detached herself. There were a few times when she had enjoyed sex with him, usually in the morning or when they were on vacation.

When they were out of town, she felt more relaxed without the structure of their usual routine. David usually got up, brought her coffee, took a shower and returned to bed. He was more likely to shave, use cologne, and try to please her by engaging in prolonged sex play prior to penetration and thrusting. Margaret felt more cared for because of the extra attention. It seemed to evoke a recip-rocal effort to give him special attention. Perhaps they departed from the married couple role and took on the role of friends and lovers, or perhaps they departed from roles entirely. Margaret seemed to feel more interest in David as a person and was more likely to share her feelings with him. She found when she did that, she was more likely to feel arousal and experience orgasm.

Toward the end of their counseling experience, they began to take three-day weekends, leaving Leslie with her grandparents. They were exploring their sexual relationship to a greater extent than they had ever done before. David enjoyed it very much when Margaret became more sexually assertive. It excited him to see her respond to his touch. Kissing her all over her body and touching her face and hair was something he rarely did at home, where most of the sexual experience involved only genital contact. Unfortunately, this intimacy was not easily sustained when they returned home. David became preoccupied with his decorating business and Margaret sought out her women friends to meet her emotional needs for closeness and nongenital touch. They had to establish more consistency.

Margaret did not think of herself as bisexual. She preferred the company of women and responded with indifference to most men. David, however, had many nonstereotypic qualities. His work as a designer and decorator gave him a special appreciation for a woman's interests. Initially, Margaret had thought David was gay, probably because she was accustomed to thinking in stereotypes, all male decorators are gay. She was surprised to discover that he was indeed straight and was attracted to her. She was not immediately attracted to him sexually and was amazed that she felt a response when he kissed and touched her. What was going on? She knew she was lesbian, there was no doubt about that. Her primary interests and fantasies were all of women. But there was something about David's personality and interest patterns that peaked her arousal. This reaction to David made it easier for Margaret to marry and live with him. However, soon after they had married, a distancing effect occurred. This seemed to begin with the division of household duties in traditional gender-specific ways. There was no rational cause for this task division since both David and Margaret had cooked, shopped, done laundry, and taken care of their own cars before they were married. They didn't talk or even think about what they were doing--it just happened. Joint tasks were divided along gender-specific lines. Gradually their relationship became stylized and role bound, so much so that their uniqueness as individuals faded. Margaret began to think of David as a man, her husband, and not as a friend. All the negative associations surrounding men that she had built up over the years seeped into her perception of him. Her arousal reaction to him, as limited as it was, also diminished. David generalized his associations with wife and mother to Margaret, treating her with so much indifference that she often thought he wouldn't notice if she disappeared entirely.

During the relationship restructuring process, they were able to laugh at themselves. David said: "I'm much better at doing laundry than Margaret. She mixes whites with pastels and then adds bleach." Margaret laughed and said, "That's not much better than you mowing the lawn in a straight line instead of at an angle, the way it's supposed to be done, the way I do it." They concluded that they didn't have to follow unwritten gender specific rules about task division. Margaret liked to mow the lawn, and David did not, so he traded it off for the laundry. Insignificant though that might seem, it gave them a sense of being themselves.

It was not so easy to resolve the deceit and infidelity issue. David did not feel that he could stay married to Margaret if she continued to relate sexually to women. He wanted a monogamous relationship. She promised she would not sexualize with women as long as David gave her more attention and provided nonsexual touch, cuddling, and longer periods of sex play prior to entering and thrusting. On the surface, it sounded like a workable compromise, but David couldn't believe that Margaret would honor her word. Nor did he believe that she could suppress her arousal response to women. This grieved him sorely. "I couldn't relate sexually to men," he said, "no matter how many compromises I made; it just wouldn't work. She will always want a woman. I'll never be enough."

Margaret had no response. In her heart she felt that this was true. David was not a woman. He could never be as nurturing, as soft, or as sweet as a woman could be. Same-sex emotional kinship is a powerful force. They were both overcome with sadness. They held each other and cried. The truth was the truth: Margaret was not heterosexual. She was lesbian and would have to renounce part of her true self if she remained in the marriage with David. David desperately wanted to believe that Margaret could change--that he could trust her and that she could love him as he wanted to be loved. Margaret wanted that too, but she doubted herself: "I've practiced deception all my life. Living as a straight woman when I'm gay is deception. Staying in the closet is deception. Being married to David is deception. Being part of the lesbian subculture when I don't feel like I belong there is deception. Is there anyplace I can go? Anyplace where I fit in?" Her voice broke and disintegrated into heaving sobs. She was slumped over in her chair. David touched her shoulder. She drew back, saying, "You can't trust me, I can't trust myself."

The intensity of that session marked a change in the reconciliation process. It was healing. The truth was out. Both felt its ugliness and its beauty. The only way they could maintain their relationship was to accept and embrace the truth. There was no assurance for either one that their marriage could go on. Neither David nor Margaret wanted the consequences of divorce for themselves or for their child. They loved one another, but certainly not in the traditional way that two people are generally expected to love one another in marriage--or did they? *What do you think? What are the real issues in this relationship dilemma?*

David and Margaret chose to restructure their relationship rather than abandon it. To do so, they had to act in accordance with the facts of who they were as real people. They could not live in accordance with an abstract concept of what a marriage should be. Emphasizing this practice rather than the theoretical or imaginary gave them more room within their marital roles to accept and respect one another. Their love was strengthened by mutual pain and anxiety. Confronting and restructuring their marriage in accordance with reality was a powerful bonding experience.

Restructuring occurs naturally and consistently in most relationships. There need not be a crisis to set it in motion. In non-consensual relationships, small children engage in restructuring attempts when they struggle for more power with their parents.

Noreen was the youngest of three children. At five, she was dominated by her older sister, Jane, who was seven, and a brother, Jerry, who was ten. Her siblings had very little patience with her and avoided her whenever possible. When she was allowed to be around them, they forced her into a very limited role. She always had to be the baby or the dog when they played house. She felt unimportant and tried to please in order to be accepted.

Her mother was busy running the house and helping Noreen's father with the family business. Noreen wanted more attention from her mother and more respect from her siblings, a formidable problem for a five-year-old. So far, nothing had worked. She had tried being good and cooperating to the best of her abilities, but the outcome had been minimal. Everyone seemed to like it when she was good because they didn't have to attend to her.

Gradually, her personality changed. Her need for attention seemed to escalate. She became anxious. She would cry hysterically if she was left alone in a room by herself. She even refused to sleep in her own bed at night. His reaction reached panic proportions: at bedtime she would cry and cling to her mother until she was allowed to sleep between her parents in their bed or on a pallet on the floor by her mother's side of the bed. She wanted to be cared for like a baby. Noreen also developed numerous physical complaints, including headaches, stomachaches and vomiting.

When it came time to enroll in school she refused to go and screamed when attempts were made to separate her from her mother. Her brother and sister were disgusted with her infantile behavior and retaliated by making fun of her and hitting her when the parents weren't around. This frightened Noreen. She developed so much fear of her siblings that she thought they would kill her. She had bunk beds in her room, and whenever she was forced to stay in her own room at night, she would change beds continually, hoping to out-maneuver her siblings whom she believed were coming to kill her.

By the time the family came in for counseling, Noreen had developed a full-blown anxiety disorder. "Noreen used to be so good you hardly knew she was around. It's only in the past couple of years that she has become so demanding." Her mother, Claire, who was exhausted with trying to cope with Noreen's behavior along with all her other responsibilities. The siblings remained impatient and disgusted. Their hostility toward Noreen grew. She sensed this and became even more anxious that they would harm her. The pictures she drew of herself and the family clearly reflected her anxiety.

In a family meeting that took place immediately after Halloween, all members were working together on a family mural. Noreen drew a picture of herself in a black pot with fire underneath it. Family members were drawn standing around cooking her. When they talked about what this meant, Noreen's brother and sister felt she was just feeling sorry for herself and being dramatic. Her father, Clint, was visibly disturbed that Noreen was so afraid of her own family. Claire cried, partially for Noreen and partially for herself because she was so tired of the whole process.

It's hard to know how much Noreen understood about the process of counseling, but it was clear she enjoyed the attention she received in session as well as the sense of being part of her family. I pointed that out: "Noreen doesn't seem to be crying or clinging when you are all together and she is included fully in the family activities." My interpretation was not lost on the family. They didn't like the idea that they were responsible for Noreen's behavior. And perhaps they were not. However, it helped for them to conceptualize Noreen as a family member rather than as the identified patient who needed "fixing" so the rest of the family could get back to business as usual.

As Noreen was gradually integrated more fully into the family, her anxiety diminished. She had fewer physical complaints and began to sleep in her own room. She was afraid of the dark and kept her lamp on all night, but she stopped switching beds. She felt more secure in general. What had happened?

This five-year-old child had successfully restructured her relationship with her family. Although she could not articulate clearly that she needed a change, she was able to act out her feelings and wrest an adjustment from her parents and siblings. Their responsivity to her needs was motivated by their own comfort level: she made life so miserable for her family that they were driven to seek outside help. Noreen was only five years old, but her predicament parallels that of many adolescents and adults who are beset with anxiety because their relationships are unsatisfying. Her symptoms, which are clearly described as "Anxiety Disorder of Infancy and Childhood" in the *DSM-IV*, were caused by the system in which she functioned. As the system adjusted, her symptoms diminished. She was fortunate that her parents and siblings were willing to make the adjustment rather than continue to see her as a disruptive force that deserved to be punished or expelled. This family made a realistic adjustment, reforming their views of themselves and each other. At the peak of the family crisis, Noreen was cast as the identified patient, the dysfunctional one. As counseling continued, it became clear that all members of the family system were contributing to the problem. Therefore, all of them had to be part of the solution.

Let's look into a relationship that was basically healthy at the outset, started to experience difficulty as most relationships do, and then developed a negative delusional quality. Barbara and Claude's sexual relationship had deteriorated, and they began to see each other through negative eyes. Awareness of each other's positive qualities diminished, and they began to develop unfavorable stereotypes about one another, so much so that they had to separate before they could let go of the negative delusions.

Barbara and Claude did not want to stay married, but they did not want a divorce. The frequency of their sexual encounters had dwindled to once every two weeks, and Barbara described them as "quick fucks" or "Archie Bunker sex." Barbara said: "His approach never varies. He gets in bed after I've been there several hours, rubs my back for two to three minutes, puts his head under the covers, maybe touches my breasts for a second or two, and then goes down on me and starts to do oral sex. After fifteen years of marriage he still doesn't know where my clitoris is, and if by chance I start to feel something, he stops and tries to force his penis into my mouth."

She spoke in an even monotone with a dead look in her eyes. Claude sat there, looking bored. He even yawned. It was hard to tell whether his reaction was indifference, bad manners, or an overworked defense system. Was it a defense against seeing himself through Barbara's eyes in a negative way?

I remember looking at him, and waiting for him to speak. Several minutes went by. I expected Barbara to start talking again before he could respond. She cleared her throat, her lips moved slightly. I continued to look at him although she tried to get my attention. It worked. Claude said: "I don't know who she's talking about. It's not me."

This was how it was with them: They had totally different perceptions of the same sexual encounter. Claude consistently denied his ineptness as a lover. He preferred to see it as Barbara's problem. A typical interchange went something like this: Claude would say, "She doesn't do her share, just lies there and expects me to give her an orgasm." Barbara then would respond, "He won't kiss me but he expects me to let him ejaculate in my mouth." She was so angry that she did not want to make love to him or share her body with him in any way.

I felt as if they were inviting me to judge them and pronounce who was in the right. Why had Barbara waited until now to express her anger? More important, why had she gone along with sex on his terms? The same question haunted Barbara. She said, looking at me: "If I hadn't been so busy protecting his ego, I would have...," her voice trailed off. There was a look of sheer despair on her face.

Much of her anger was directed inward. She hated herself for faking orgasm, and for having sex just for the closeness--pretending it meant more to her than it really did. I remember her calling and asking for an individual session so she could talk about her anger toward herself without furnishing her mate, Claude, with ammunition to use against her. I explained that I preferred to meet with both of them. I had to teach them to communicate, which would take much longer if we met individually. I wanted to try conjoint sessions first.

Barbara tried to convince me that joint sessions wouldn't work: "He won't listen. When we disagree he states his position and then turns on the radio or TV so I can't respond." She needed to break through his defenses and establish her right to be heard. Barbara didn't have much hope that it would work, but she did agree to forgo individual sessions in favor of conjoint meetings. It was slow, hard work. She had great difficulty overcoming female role behavior. Like many women, she cried when she was angry. Was this convoluted response an enculturated effort to engender a feeling of mercy or guilt in her male adversary, or was it simply frustration because she wasn't strong enough to kill him?

There were many times when she wanted to kill him. She reported having fantasies that he would have a fatal accident when he traveled or when he was late coming home from work. Her husband was stunned when he was confronted with the force of her hatred. "She really wants me dead. I can't believe she feels that way about me. I thought we were doing better, especially since we've been coming to see you."

I decided to model direct statements for Barbara and said: "It seems odd that you are surprised. Maybe she's right, you don't listen." I was speaking in a low voice and making direct eye contact. He didn't like it. His jaw tightened. He got up and started to move toward the door saying, "This isn't doing any good." I maintained my position, "This is why Barbara hates you." He spun around, facing me: "Fuck you very much! I don't come here to be insulted!" I continued: "You're not listening. You want to avoid learning the truth." As he looked at me, I continued speaking in a softer voice: "Listen, Claude, listen. You can handle this. The truth will not hurt you." He corrected me; "Your version of the truth, not mine." It was the opening I wanted, so I replied, "Let's compare our versions of the truth."

It was a conciliatory response. I had conceded that there was a way for his truth to be known. He sensed acceptance. Sitting down, he looked at Barbara, who had remained silent during the entire interchange between us. She did have a little smile on her face. She looked at Claude and said, "I don't really hate you, at least not all of the time. What's your version of truth?" And so it began--they started to talk. He said, "You won't have sex with me." Barbara replied, "There's nothing in it for me. Whenever I'm in the mood, you're unwilling. But you expect me to respond when you haven't bathed, brushed your teeth, or even spoken to me for hours. Do you have any idea how you smell? One part alcohol, one part stale cigarette smoke, and one part garlic. Add day old sweat on your clothes. Makes me sick!"

Claude was outraged and embarrassed: "That's not true! You're making me sound like a slob. That's not me." Turning to me, he said: "This is why I can't listen to her. She's lying." My response did not please him: "I wonder why she sees you that way. Does any of it fit your perception of your grooming habits, even slightly?" I was trying to circumvent his defenses.

Of course, Claude said, "NO!" I just looked at him in silence, raising one eyebrow slightly. He reconsidered: "Well, I do smoke and I usually have a drink every night." Barbara interrupted triumphantly: "A drink? You drink steadily from the moment you get home until you come to bed."

I directed my gaze toward her momentarily and shook my head no. "Not now Barbara. Let Claude clarify his thoughts about the grooming issue." Returning my attention to Claude. "So you see how you might smell like tobacco and alcohol?" He nodded yes and looked down. I didn't belabor the point and he apparently felt safe. I had protected him from Barbara's attack on his drinking. Choicepoint. Should I pursue the issue of drinking or continue to organize the exploration around their sexual encounters? I decided not to focus on the issue of alcohol, knowing it would come up again in their discussion of their sexual encounters.

I looked at Barbara: "Can you say something about your own bedroom grooming?" Barbara flushed: "Not as bad as his, but I don't take a bubble bath, and put on a black nightie if that's what you mean." This was Claude's cue to interrupt: "She sleeps in sweats and doesn't shower until she gets up in the morning." I asked him if that affected his arousal response. There was a long silence. Claude sighed deeply and started to talk. "Actually, she always looks good and smells good." Barbara looked up. She seemed surprised and somewhat pleased he saw her that way.

It was the first positive statement he had made about her. I remained silent. Barbara took my cue and gave Claude the time he needed to gather his thoughts. I was elated. I thought we were home free--but it's not that easy to dispel a negative stereotype.

Claude sensed he had given too much ground: "I'm a good lover or she has been faking it all these years. I spend lots of time trying to give her an orgasm. I don't believe her. She just wants to hurt me." Barbara shook her head no. She was tired of his defensiveness and seemed ready to end the session and perhaps the relationship.

They came back on a weekly basis for several months, talking despondently about their relationship and how dead it was sexually. It was unclear whether they were moving toward divorce or a healthier marriage, but they started to see each other a little differently. The negative delusion seemed to be fading. Their sexual encounters increased and Claude made a real effort to please his wife sexually. It worked, but she could not forget his previous indifference or the multitude of insults she had endured throughout their marriage. Even though sex was better and she responded to him with more affection and humor, there was underlying bitterness and mistrust.

Barbara continued to raise negative issues. She had a great deal of old anger and resentment to express before the negative delusion she had constructed around Claude would fade. "I hate to go to parties with him or let him around my friends or work associates. He flirts so obviously it's embarrassing. Whenever there's a young girl around he acts like an adolescent."

So it went, week after week. Claude's anger was spent, he had let go of it. He gradually let down his defenses and began to see himself through Barbara's eyes. He was appalled and truly motivated to change, but the process had altered Barbara also. She had also gotten an unflattering glimpse of herself. She saw herself as a victim, a spineless victim who had tolerated abusive behavior from her spouse.

Instead of feeling validated when Claude acknowledged his insensitive treatment of her, it increased her anger. Barbara hated herself for taking it so long, and began to feel that she could never relate to him again. "I can't believe I was such a wimp. I should have walked out long ago."

As long as Claude defended himself and denied his mistreatment of her, Barbara had a goal--to convince him that she was right and he was wrong. With this accomplished, she no longer felt any purpose in the marriage. She moved out of the home they had shared for fifteen years and filed for divorce. Claude continued to pursue her. They both dated other people and continued to relate to each other as friends. Neither one pushed the settlement process or pressured their attorneys for a court date.

About eighteen months later, they reconciled. It took them that long to dispel the delusion and reinstate positive, realistic views of one another. Even though their relationship had faltered, they did not abandon it.

This marriage relationship is representative in many ways of all relationships, not just love and sexual relationships, but all basic family ties. Parent-child, sibling, grandparent-grandchild: virtually every relationship has its stereotypic role prescriptions that govern and restrict the expectations, and satisfaction levels derived from them.

Culturally induced delusions regarding what to expect and how to act make it difficult to see, experience, and appreciate those we relate to as real people. Instead, we take on roles and expect our counterpart in the relationships to fit neatly into the idealized version. We want the ideal so desperately that we delude ourselves, and when the delusion fades, we discount reality.

At this juncture it is generally possible to restructure the relationship along more realistic lines. This is true for both consensual and non-consensual relationships. Restructuring relationships seems to be a natural impulse. Noreen, the five- year-old child, felt this impulse when she began to act out and express her anxiety regarding how she was treated by her family. Her symptoms, or negative behavior, created a disturbance in the family system but served the purpose of accomplishing change and reformation of family relationships. Disturbances in relationships often offer an opportunity for positive restructuring. Delusional relationships can benefit from such disturbances.

Chapter 9

The Magic Ingredient

Magic is usually defined as hocus-pocus, deception, or artful trickery. There are associations with ritual and the invocation of the supernatural, and overpowering influences. Is this the stuff magic is made of? Is sexual chemistry magic? Overblown lust that burns us to the bone and preoccupies our thoughts? Is magic the discovery of a new body? The opportunity for us to present a mysterious and beautiful persona that captivates, entrances, and deludes.

Magic moments in relationships--how do we define them? Looking into the eyes of a sweetheart over a champagne cocktail? Watching a son run across a field and score a touchdown? Are they the moments when the strength of our love and bonding surpasses disappointment, pain, and boredom that has characterized our relationships? The moments when we feel pride in ourselves and our loved ones for overcoming difficult situations? Shared moments of pride and self-confidence? Sounds too simple to be called magic, but maybe these are enchanted moments. It depends on your expectations.

In families, is magic approximating the stereotypes of the perfect parent, the perfect child, the storybook big brother or little sister? In friendship, is it always being there, always listening and understanding, always being ready to help? The romantic true blue friend. In business, is it giving a hundred and one percent--skipping lunch breaks, working weekends, and finally getting acknowledged for it? Is it coming up with that great idea at just the right time, or is it refusing to sacrifice your life for the corporation? Is magic the power to step out of a cookie-cutter image and confront the reality of truth? What is magic? Let's think about it.

A child's idea of magic usually includes wish fulfillment. Like having a genie with supernatural powers. Miracles which make the bad go away and everything feel all right.

Noah wanted to fly, but he did not have wings. Every Sunday when he went to church, he would ask God to give him wings and on Monday morning he would check his shoulders for signs of wing development. It never happened. By the time he was eight, he had given up. He knew he would never grow wings and soar like a bird. It didn't matter. He didn't believe in magic anymore, and he didn't believe in God anymore either. As far as Noah was concerned, God was a myth like Santa Claus and the Easter Bunny. Noah and his folks still played the silly game of the Tooth Fairy. He went along with it to get the money, but he knew his parents put the dollar under pillow and took his tooth. He was only eight years old, and he no longer believed in magic, Santa Claus, the Easter Bunny, the Tooth Fairy, or even God. He had experienced one disappointment after another--he couldn't tell them apart.

What the disappointments had in common was that adults in his life had told him about these various supernatural beings which had all turned out to be untrue. We can smile at Noah's childlike innocence or we can speculate on the miseducation that we impose on young. Our current system of education allows children to sort these concepts out on their own, arriving at their own conclusions regarding the perceptions and conceptualizations. Do we really want them to equate Santa Claus with God? Can't we be more specific about gradations of the supernatural?

We do not listen to children like Noah and clarify what misunderstandings may be occurring. We do not check to see if what we, as adults, communicate to them is fully understood. Noah, at age eight, knew that magic wasn't true and neither was prayer. He also knew that God, Santa Claus, the Easter Bunny, and the Tooth Fairy had all been presented to him as having supernatural power. All untrue. This imprecise method of education resulted in confusion about the concept of magic. Children have difficulty separating reality from fable; so do many adults.

Returning to the original association of magic with wish fulfillment, we can understand how and why we are all vulnerable to delusional thinking. We want something to be true, even when we know it is unlikely or even impossible. We yearn for magic to make our lives easier, happier, and more fun. In that pursuit, we often lose sight of the beauty of truth and reality. The power of truth, simply stated, lives on forever. It does not fade, as delusions do. A simple statement of truth can bring tears to one's eyes and transform a dilemma into a magical outcome. Let's redefine magic.

Jimmy was in the process of demystifying his relationship with his best friend, Jack. They worked for the same company and had started there at about the same time. Now, their immediate supervisor was leaving and a promotion from within was expected. Of the two, Jimmy needed the promotion more financially because his wife was pregnant and they already had trouble meeting their monthly bills. Jack was single and very dependent on his career for his self-esteem. Both men were qualified. They were worried about the impact of the decision on their relationship. They had been friends for years and had supported one another through many life crises. Jack had been Jimmy's best man and would probably be the child's godfather--unless the competitiveness of the promotion dilemma destroyed their friendship.

Jimmy saw himself as more vulnerable: "Jack is my best friend, my only real male friend. He's got other buddies but since I've been married, I've dropped out of circulation. Most of the other guys aren't interested in hanging with an old married man. And I don't see much chance for me to make new friends, that are just mine, you know, outside the couple stuff. Jack and I go way back. We smoked our first joint together--and quit using at about the same time. It's not going to be the same without him." I reflected his feeling: "You sound as if you're already grieving the loss of Jack's friendship."

"It's already changing. We used to share our leads and cover for each other. Now we don't do that. We'll be judged on the basis of our total sales. Top man wins." As he spoke, his shoulders slumped and his voice dropped. He described how, the previous month, for the first time, he had let excess leads grow cold rather than give them to Jack, as he had always done before. "I need that promotion. We need the money, but I feel like I'm screwing my best friend." He stopped talking, looked at me, and asked, "What are you thinking?" "You're hurting," I responded quietly. He went on: "Maybe I should quit my job, move on and try for a better job in a new company. I can't see myself supervising Jack or working for him. We've always been peers. What a shitty deal." I suggested he invite Jack to come in and talk about it, since their communication was becoming so strained that it affected their productivity at work as well as their personal relationship. Jimmy didn't like the idea and said that Jack wouldn't go for it. I was surprised when both men came in for Jimmy's next scheduled session.

They were both grinning. I suspected that they were high, either on pot or maybe alcohol, but I couldn't smell anything. When I asked, they denied it, so we went on and conducted our meeting. It was hard to get them focused. They had decided to both quit and go into business together, saying that neither one of them wanted to win out over the other. I asked them to disclose the negative feelings that had been accumulating since the announcement of the impending promotion.

Jack spoke first: "I knew you had extra leads and sacked them. It made me mad. I wouldn't have done that to you." Jimmy looked down, studying his fingernails while the clock ticked interminably. Finally Jimmy replied: "I'm an asshole. I'm not proud of it. You take the job. I don't want it." Jack's mood changed: "I'm not Mr. Clean. You got a couple of messages I didn't give you." Jimmy looked up, "No shit? I'm glad I'm not the only dickhead around." They both laughed, their eyes moist--these men loved each other.

I was struck by their dependence on locker room jargon. The friends really cared about each other and were having a hard time staying in the male stereotype while expressing their feelings. I decided not to comment on it, as it might inhibit them further if they knew I could see their feelings so clearly. Also, it was not the time for a teachy-preachy lecture on gender-restricted communication. The session ended with the men hugging each other and scheduling another meeting the following week. They canceled that session. It was several months before I knew the outcome. Jimmy got the promotion and Jack received a promotion and transfer to a southern branch office.

The magic in that session lived on in my mind. After exposing their mutual weaknesses, the men faced their dilemma together. Unable to resolve it, they confirmed their relationship. The anguish of the shared dilemma evoked a magical moment of truth and union. Their friendship was not destroyed by the stereotypic pressure of the male proscription to achieve. I was very touched by the bond between these two men and their ability to express their feelings. There is little doubt that an overpowering and mysterious bond had been formed between them. Perhaps we should integrate this feeling into our definition of magic: Something unusual had occurred when the friends acknowledged their feelings for each other.

Mothering was not magic for Nancy. She did not like children. The constant drain of attending to their physical needs and answering their questions evoked a throbbing resentment. Why did her life have to be so limited? She had married and given birth before she knew there were other options. She was quite intelligent and interested in becoming a researcher or working in a bookstore, where she could then indulge her habit of skimming publications of all kinds and returning to the text to ascertain if she had comprehended the content of the volume. She liked to be alone. She liked to think about herself and her own feelings. She did not enjoy exchanges with "unformed minds" as she found nothing exciting in that experience. Her children ranged from ages three to eleven, with a middle child of seven. They were not pleasant children. They had picked up their mother's habit of swearing and using vulgar images to vent hostility. They all seemed desperate to receive attention of any kind. During their counseling appointment times, the rest of the staff tried not to schedule because their behaviors were so destructive and distracting. Even though we gave them guidelines for behavior while they were in the Counseling Center, everyone heaved a sigh of relief when the "exodus" occurred. The waiting room was littered with torn magazines and candy wrappers after their visits.

Nancy couldn't control her children, sometimes they upset her so much she would even leave, walking outside to have a cigarette. Oddly enough, they quieted down when she departed. Perhaps their incessant misbehavior was designed to evoke a response from her. All they usually got was cursing or threats. "I wasn't meant to be a mom," she said. "I'm so pissed at their father, that stupid prick. He drinks all day, leaving me to care for his fucking kids." I asked her to clean up her mouth. I explained that it was bad for the children and it also distracted me. Try as I did, I couldn't bracket my distaste for her language, and I finally suggested that she find another counselor who could stomach her language. She was incredulous. "I thought the customer was always right!" she retorted, wrinkling her nose at me. "I've read Carl Rogers. You are supposed to have unconditional positive regard for your clients." My response was totally authentic. "Sorry, Nancy, I just can't fake it. I find your language offensive. I don't like hearing it coming from your children either. I think you can communicate without evoking offensive images, but it's your choice. I'm sure you can find a counselor who will accept it." I stood up, as I always did when the session was over. Nancy started to cry in a plaintive, childlike manner: "Don't leave me. I'll do anything you say. Just don't leave me."

I felt manipulated. Her regressed state irritated me. I had actually been looking forward to eliminating her and her children from my client load, but her desperation touched me. I sighed audibly: "Okay, Nancy. We'll try it a little longer." She never cussed again in session, and I also noticed a change in the way she handled the children, she was less combative. Months later, she told me that my confrontation of her language was a turning point for her. "You were so honest and you had the self-respect to tell me how you felt. I knew you really cared. No one's ever called me on my behavior the way you have. I was able to do the same thing with my kids. And they respected me for it, too." It was an important lesson. I had set realistic limits for Nancy's behavior by speaking the truth and modeling my adherence to it. I was struck by the almost magical power this had on the course of therapy. As I reflect on counseling relationships, I realize that Nancy and I had transcended the role of client and counselor during that interchange. It was more than clinical confrontation that brought about the change in Nancy's behavior. It was the magical power of truth between two people. What kind of magic is that? Certainly not trickery or deception. But the pure, unadorned truth, presented in such a manner that the heart and intellect are engaged rather than the defenses. Relationship truth cannot be accepted if it comes in the form of an attack. When presented simply, in a moderate tone of voice, the truth of the message penetrates both external and internal defenses, touching the core of self-knowledge. Affirmation is painful but growth inducing.

Unfortunately, much of what we learn about interpersonal relating and communication encourages deceit and duplicity. There are times when truth is used as a weapon, and it can create havoc in relationships.

Mildred and Virgil, a biracial couple, struggled consistently with their truth and how to absorb it, and generate a positive result in their marriage. Virgil vacillated between being proud of his Afro-American heritage and despising himself for being black. There were many obstacles he had to overcome in the racist society in which he lived and worked. He was a tall, good-looking man with natural presence. He had a soft voice and presented himself as if he was at ease at all times in the white environment. It was a lie. He was always aware of reactions to his color, regardless of how subtle. His law firm valued his services. He was more than a token. His colleagues respected the way he handled himself whenever he was denied access to opportunity because of his color, which happened often.

One time the firm sponsored a golf tournament in an exclusive country club. The word came down that Virgil would not be welcome. He objected to the discrimination. His position was that the firm should withdraw its support of the tournament and not participate. This did not occur. Virgil wrote a memo and circulated it throughout the firm stating that it was poor policy for the firm to acquiesce to racial discrimination. Virgil asked for support through nonattendance. There was no response. Two days before the tournament, Virgil was given an important case that necessitated him being out of town during the event. He was not surprised, but he took the case and did an exceptionally good job on it.

When we talked about it, Virgil explained how he was able to deal with this bigotry and continue to function. He remained optimistic and said that the day would come when the firm would stand behind him publicly. He denied his anger and said he felt none. His new case was a plum, a consolation prize, more important than forcing the discrimination issue right now. Virgil was a nice guy. He believed in the American dream. He worked and won many people over to his side. He maintained strong ties with his family, although he did not live in the black community. He bought a house in white suburbia and seemed to get along with his neighbors. He dated both white and black women. When he did marry Mildred, a white woman, he was confident that everything would work out, even though neither of their families expressed support of the marriage. Their wedding was not well attended. In spite of the fact that they both had large families, only a few members from each side came. Mildred was hurt and surprised. She had been enchanted by Virgil's self-confidence and success. During the courtship period they had visited different members of their respective families and no active rejection had occurred. They received polite indifference. Mildred felt they would be more welcomed after the wedding. Virgil was accustomed to polite indifference and he had developed a defense against it. He also had believed Mildred to be more capable of tolerating it than she was. He had made the assumption that she would take on his mode of defense and that together they would overcome all obstacles. Mildred had had no idea there would be so many problems. Although they had talked about the difficulties of biracial marriages and had read a few articles on how to cope with a black and white world, she was in no way prepared for what she experienced as ostracism.

"Virgil seemed so happy and confident, like it was easy to be black in a white world. Most people seemed to accept us. I never dreamed it would be so hard." The tears came, but with very little sound. Virgil was sitting next to her on the couch and he put his arm around her. She stiffened slightly. He looked at me. He was afraid he was losing her. I said nothing. Mildred went on, "It's not like you lied to me, but you didn't tell me it would be so hard." "I thought you knew," he said. "I thought you could handle it. It gets easier." "Easier? You don't care any more; only I care. I care that my family doesn't invite us for any of the birthdays or other occasions when they get together." She was sobbing now, loudly, and shouting. Virgil's fear mounted. He had miscalculated and things were getting out of control. He didn't know if he could fix it. "What do I do, Doc?" I looked at him and said, "Let's get all the feelings out and then we can see the options more clearly." He closed his eyes. That was not what he wanted to hear. He wanted me to help Mildred get past her fear. He didn't want her to explore it as he was afraid that might make it bigger. He wanted less, not more feeling: Virgil wanted magic, the supernatural kind that has an overpowering influence over natural events. I had no magic wand, only the ability to guide the couple in facing reality and understanding fully what was involved if they were to continue their marriage. That was the basic issue: Mildred didn't want to be married to an Afro-American if it was going to be so unbearably painful. She was terrified of having children, and having them feel the discrimination she was beginning to feel. Virgil was stunned. He didn't want a divorce or an annulment. This was his first major encounter with a situation he could not endure or change. His defenses were severely shaken.

In previous crisis situations, he had managed to continue working at his usual high level of competence, remaining calm and purposeful but Mildred's reaction to polite indifference was something he had not expected. His equanimity had been breached. He looked and acted differently. He had no answers. He felt as if all he could do was wait: he was at her mercy. Mildred didn't recognize him. Where was his confidence, his strength, his power to overcome? They were nowhere in evidence. What Mildred saw was a desperate, frightened man who was unable to reassure her that everything would be all right. All he said was: "I'm sorry. I've hurt you. I didn't know it would be this way." He was talking about her reaction, not the pressure from the extended families and the outside world. He had duped himself, and perhaps her as well, by pretending that their biracial match would be accepted, just because he wanted it so badly. "I still think it will work," he said. "All we have to do is hang tight and everyone will get used to it." He looked at her pleadingly: "Give it a chance."

His attitude infuriated Mildred. "That's fine for you to say. You have everything to gain and I have everything to lose." Virgil didn't respond. Perhaps he felt that what she said was true. She had gone from a position of acceptance in the community to one of being marginally tolerated. She felt as if people only tolerated her and her marriage to Virgil. She had lost her social prestige and security. He, on the other hand, had gained a "trophy wife," a white woman, who would enhance his status in the community. This was how she saw it, at least until he told her how it really felt to him, revealing what lay beneath the facade, which she had never seen. "I don't fit in either community now. My family sees me as a traitor--an Oreo--for leaving the community, marrying a white woman, turning my back on Afro-Americanism and taking my education, my money, and my success to Whitesville. I have no one left but you."

"I don't feel sorry for you," she said. "Maybe I should, but I don't. You made a choice, freely, I didn't. I had stars in my eyes and you knew it. I feel like you're using me on your big ascendancy upward from the black ghetto to white suburbia, with little Mildred, stupid little Mildred, as a stepping stone."

Harsh words--were they true? Did Virgil know what he was doing to Mildred's life when he married her? Did it matter? Wasn't she responsible for the choice she had made? Mildred didn't think so. As far as she was concerned, it had not been informed choice. "I didn't know what I was getting into. Not only did Virgil misrepresent himself, but my friends and my family also led me to believe it would be all right. Nothing much would change, except that we would be married and living together. No one told me we would be ignored and excluded." She went over this again and again, placing the responsibility outside of herself for the choice she had made. Repetition was necessary: She had to repeat it in order to integrate the truth. There are no short-cuts in therapy. We retraced the same material while Mildred vented her feelings and desensitized herself to what had happened in her life.

Virgil had reached a point where he just listened to her. He did not try to defend himself or confront her rationalizations. After three months of weekly meetings, he was ready to end the relationship. "I'll do the paperwork and file for annulment. We can't go on like this." Mildred said, "Good!" Then she got up and walked to the door. Turning, she looked back at us. "We should have done this long ago instead of spending ninety dollars an hour to make fools of ourselves in front of you." She walked out and the door clicked closed. There were no tears in Virgil's eyes. He asked me, "Do you think I duped her?" "No," I said, "You were a little optimistic, though." He said, "Yeah, I think I saw her as a part of me rather than as her own person, with her own reactions."

"I wonder if it would make a difference if she could hear you say that. She's been trying to force an admission from you for months."   "I don't think it would matter," he said, "Mildred's pretty dependent on her family and not having them around has been rough. Little ole black me is not enough to make up for losing them."

We were both surprised when Mildred called and arranged a family session in my office. There were fourteen people there besides myself, and Virgil was the only non-white. Mildred's goal for the session was to tell everyone in her family how she felt. I was impressed that everyone had attended. We sat in a circle, with some people on the floor. Mildred explained how she didn't know what she was doing when she married Virgil. She felt she owed everyone an apology. She was also angry at everyone, including me, for not warning her. There wasn't much response as this group was not accustomed to self-disclosure. Mildred's father said, "You made your bed--lie in it." Not very comforting. Her mother and sisters cried. Mildred may have realized that there was no turning back. Her family was not going to welcome Virgil with open arms--but they weren't casting her out, either. She had to do it alone.

About ten minutes before the session was over, Mildred said that she intended to stay married to Virgil if he would have her. She would face the world, including her family, with a determination not to be destroyed. This dramatic turn of events still evoked no response from the family. Virgil didn't look surprised. Apparently the couple had talked about it before the session and temporarily resolved their issues. They hadn't bothered to inform me ahead of time, but it didn't matter. Content is not important. What was significant was that the truth was spoken, reality was faced, and the magic ingredient was once more at work. What had changed? All delusions had been stripped away. Secret feelings had been expressed. Mildred and Virgil saw each other as they really were and their position in the world as it really was. It wasn't any less formidable, but self-knowledge and truth gave them power to go on. That's magic.

Acknowledgment of truth provides an exit from seemingly unworkable situations. The silent attendance of Mildred's family at our session is symbolic of their position. She was still part of their unit, which they acknowledged by sitting in my office and listening to her feelings. They could not speak because they had nothing to say, but the women's tears expressed the shared pain of the family. Virgil was awed by the curious blend of resistance and acceptance signified by the family's presence at the meeting. Mildred's decision rested on her determination to be true to herself. She wasn't sure she loved Virgil enough to go through with being married to him, and she was afraid. But she was more afraid of betraying herself. She still didn't understand why she had married Virgil. She had been blinded by love, and now she was amazed at her own naivete. How could she have expected her family to accept her marriage to a black man without having difficulties? If the country couldn't integrate in over a hundred years, how could she expect her family to accept Virgil in one year? There had been a certain amount of self-deception in Mildred's perception of the world during the romance and courtship phase of their relationship. When the delusion faded, reality had to be faced and accepted. Encountering reality provided an opportunity for the power of truth to prevail. There was no guarantee of a happy ending or a life without pain, but the magic ingredient for Mildred was a feeling of empowerment.

It seems to be more commonplace to seek the magic of delusion than to seek the magic of truth. Substance abuse furnishes many examples of how people seek to delude themselves in order to avoid the pain of truth, regardless of its empowering characteristics.

Terri was nineteen years old. Both her parents were substance abusers. Her mother, Sherri, alternated between pot and alcohol in order to distract herself from the lack of accomplishment in her life. Terri's father, Sam, used harder drugs. He had been arrested and served time for possession and sale of illegal substances. This had happened when Terri was quite young, still in grade school. Her parents then divorced, and she lived with her mother, who struggled to support herself and her daughter.

It was a hard life. Sherri used substance to create the illusion of well-being. However, the substance-induced delusion was not powerful enough. It didn't work. She alternated between depression and anger. The only time she felt good was immediately after a drink or lighting up. There were many arguments between Terri and her mother. Sherri didn't want her daughter to follow in her footsteps, but she was too defensive to admit the truth, even when Terri confronted her with the negative example she was setting.

Terri had started abusing illegal substances when she was thirteen. She was deeply ashamed of her parent's habits, but felt compelled to emulate them. At nineteen she was arrested and referred to a diversion program for first time offenders. Terri was the single legal adult in a car full of younger high school students who had been stopped for speeding. The arresting officer found marijuana in a zip-lock bag in the glove compartment. It really didn't belong to Terri, but the car was her's. She felt lucky to plea-bargain for possession without the additional charge of contributing to the delinquency of minors.

When Terri's parents learned of her arrest, they were furious first at the authorities, and then at Terri for causing problems in the family. They chose not to see their own part in Terri's problem. To do so would have been too painful. They truly loved their daughter and couldn't bear to face the truth about how they had failed her. They had managed to maintain their delusion that they were acceptable parents and that it was the legal system that was at fault for outlawing pot.

Terri's arrest put a sizable crack in her parents' defense system. It came out in the investigations that both Sherri and Sam had allowed their daughter and her underage friends to smoke pot in their respective homes. Family counseling was recommended and they ended up in session with some of my training associates. I was struck with how desperately they struggled to maintain their delusionary system and avoid contact with reality. They were intelligent people and sensed that their whole world was about to change.

The first major change came when Sherri discovered that she had lung cancer. It gave her something else about which to be angry and depressed. It was hard to keep the sessions focused on any single issue. Fortunately, content is not a primary concern in therapy. Instead, the process of exploring and integrating feelings is what matters. Improving of the communication system is usually more important than the specific issue involved.

Terri and her parents learned how to transfer their communication skills from one topic to another. They also learned how to explore their feelings first regarding substance abuse, and later about Sherri's struggle with cancer.

Gradually, they began to face the truth. It was not by choice--their other options had been closed down. The family's defenses were confronted in counseling. They were not allowed to rant about the irrationality of government control of substances. Instead, they were guided to look at, and experience, their feelings about their habits and the effect on their lives.

Sam was the first to make the shift from avoidance to acceptance of his responsibility. This had a momentous effect on other family members. My colleague in training had targeted Sam, believing that if he acknowledged his own responsibility and made a change, the others would follow. Even though this was a divorced family, the mystique of paternalism was still apparent. Sam was asked if he thought he had any power to help his daughter and ex-wife heal their relationship.

This was a strategic question. The core of disagreement between mother and daughter was substance abuse. Terri had given up trying to get her mother to quit the habit and had taken on her mother's substance abuse pattern. They fought constantly about other issues but never focused on the core issue of Sherri's contribution to her daughter's substance abuse. Sherri never admitted she was responsible. Instead, she described herself as permissive regarding Terri's use of illegal substance. She never volunteered information about her own habit.

Sam wanted them both to quit. He could see how it was ruining their lives but was unable to effectively confront them because of his own substance abuse. When asked if he had power to help them, he knew the truth: The only way he could help them was to quit himself. Otherwise, he would have no influence over their behavior. His situation was similar to that of Sherri, his ex-wife, about whom he still cared.

Sherri did not want Terri to become an addict, but neither was she strong enough to quit, so she avoided the issue and hid from the truth as long as she could. Sam's answer to the question was initially negative: "Hell, I can't even help myself, how can I help them?" No response came from anyone. Silence--oppressive silence--filled the room. Each of them could have been thinking the same thing. None of them had been able to help himself, herself, or each other. Nothing could be truer--or more negative. I felt depression seeping through the room once more, and there was a lot of sighing. Terri tied her shoelaces in an attempt to alleviate the tension in the room. The rest of us keep looking at Sam--including Sherri, who wanted him to save her. Tears rolled out of Sam's eyes and his nose started to run, a common occurrence in sessions like these. I wasn't expecting anything.

Then Sam spoke again. "Well, for what is's worth, I'm going through detox again. This time I'll do it right, stay with it, go to the meetings, get a sponsor, the whole damn thing. Someone has gotta do something. These stupid sessions aren't gonna do it!" Sherri and her daughter looked at each other as if to ask the question, "Shall we go for it, too?" They verbalized nothing. For a moment, I felt the magic. I knew the problem wasn't over and that they had a lot of hard work to do, but I felt more hope for this family than I ever had before.

They all went through detox and rehabilitation again, but not together. Sherri and Terri went through an in house treatment program together and went on to participate in a twelve-step program, while Sam worked his program out-of-state where he could continue working as a heavy equipment repairman for farm machinery. He also went to Alcoholics Anonymous (AA) meetings. I'm not sure how many times they went out or otherwise faltered in their programs before they achieved sobriety, but I do know that the family session in which Sam spoke was highly significant. Sherri and Terri were inspired by his determination, but the single most important factor was his willingness to speak the truth and face it. It thrilled them emotionally. It was a magic feeling, which empowered them. Truth is magic.

PART II

ENCOUNTERING RELATIONSHIP DELUSION

Demystifying

Chapter 10

Demystifying Delusion

After consideration of the case studies in this text, you conclude that you are currently involved in a delusional relationship. You may even fear that delusion characterizes all of your relationships. You want to evaluate and modify your relationships. You want to know more about those factors that have affected your relating behaviors. You wonder what you should look for.

We need not delve deeply into Freudian theory to ascertain that the vast majority of our behaviors are not consciously determined. Preconscious factors govern attraction and mate selection. Learned responses from past relationships come to the surface and inappropriately affect present relationships. Reflect on how that affects our view of reality and our perceptions of self and others: An awareness of ourselves and our surroundings is clearly dependent on our past experiences. Memories of those experiences affect us at a preconscious level. Behaviors and attitudes developed in our family of origin are reenacted on a daily basis in our current relationships.

Our behaviors are also managed by external controls, which are also out of our awareness. Impressions of other people are formed on the basis of very limited information. Our interest is cued by symbols that mislead us. Symbols are not truly representative of what they stand for. The case study, in Chapter 1, of Mark and Kelly involving attraction, exemplifies this phenomena. Kelly attracted Mark by presenting herself as a warm and sexual person. The centrality of warmth as a positive trait was established by Solomon Asch as early as 1946. People are attracted to others who appear warm. One can appear warm without actually being warm. However, one hardly has to consult the research to clarify that a warm and smiling countenance attracts, while a cold and scowling one does not.

How does a warm and smiling countenance affect us?   Let's look at Gutherie's law of association (1952). If one thing has accompanied another in the past, an association will be formed. If we have previously linked positive qualities with warmth, we will do so again in the future. Mark previously associated popularity, humor, and fun with warmth and smiles. When he saw Kelly at a party, her smile was warm. That drew forth from his memory many positive associations, which he affixed to Kelly, who, of course, knew that this would occur.   Kelly successfully managed Mark's impression of her by activating cues which she could predict would evoke a favorable response. Many people understand this basic information about how to send out a cue that will attract and lure others. This can occur with or without their conscious knowledge. The impression Mark formed of Kelly illustrates how judgment can be affected externally without the knowledge or consent of the person forming the judgement.

A further note about impression management: This is a topic which we should all know more about. To increase our own awareness of how our attitudes and judgments can be externally controlled, we can familiarize ourselves with historic strategies that have consistently been employed to attract and delude, and that we ourselves use to attract and delude others.

Countless methods are employed for this purpose, not just by marketing specialists trying to sell a product but also by relationship counterparts who are seeking to manage or manipulate our reactions to them.   It is important to clarify the techniques to which you are most susceptible.

Supplication is the emphasis of one's own shortcomings and dependence and is designed to make the seduced person feel powerful and sympathetic. This might work with Joshua, who was described in the case study in the Introduction of this volume. He felt inadequate as a male and sought a female counterpart who would build him up at her own expense. This method would support his dependence on the concept of male superiority. Supplication is a strategy favored by those who feel powerless.

Self-promotion emphasizes the seducer's positive characteristics and accomplishments. Stan, our case study of the successful American dream in Chapter 7, utilized this method successfully in his ascent from a low economic status to the upper middle class. He seduced Sarah, his wife, into seeing him as competent and skillful. Stan did possess these qualities, but he failed to reveal other characteristics which he believed would make a less favorable impression. He was engaging in self-promotion.

Intimidation involves acting in a threatening manner, either physically or verbally, in an effort to control or gain power over another. Joanne, in the Chapter 2, our case study of an employee who attempted to intimidate her supervisor by threatening to quit at a crucial time when her services were needed to meet a deadline, illustrates this method. Intimidation is also a common method that males use to sexually harass females (The case of Mary, in Chapter 2).

Ingratiation is a method whereby the seducer agrees with, compliments, or gives gifts in hopes of being liked and accepted. This common method was used by Noreen, the five-year-old described in Chapter 8. It was an unsuccessful attempt to obtain more attention and power in her family. Ingratiation figures largely in prescribed female role behavior. Molly, the suicidal sixteen-year-old described in Chapter 3, was struggling to integrate this method into her adolescent identity even though it did not fit with her personality. Barry, the nontraditional male described in Chapter 5, was successful in his use of ingratiation with his girlfriend, Marla. His ability to agree with her and avoid conflict ingratiated him in that relationship.

Exemplification, the assumption of a holier-than-thou or martyr position as a method to elevate oneself to the appearance of moral worthiness, is illustrated by Mildred, the white woman who chose a biracial marriage described in Chapter 9. She adopted this method to shield herself from the fact that she had made an uninformed decision about her marriage to an Afro-American.

These methods, which are designed to make impressions and influence judgments, are extremely common. As simplistic as they might be, they have been successfully employed for thousands of years in countless human relationships. On occasion, the target person recognizes that a seductive maneuver is in process, but for the most part, however, these management techniques operate at a preconscious level. When we combine this type of external control with the fact that our responses are also affected by our past experiences and what we have learned from them, we are again faced with the obvious truth that our behaviors, thoughts and feelings are not consciously determined.

Can we actually exercise free choice in relationship formation without an awareness of how various forces shape our responses? Clearly we can not. It would, however, be possible for individuals in relationships to exercise more conscious awareness if our educational system included consistent information drawn from social psychology. Broadening the knowledge base of all learners regarding the forces that govern behavior in relationships would minimize the occurrence of preconscious choices.

Learning about gender-based role taking is a gradual process which starts in infancy. After the age of thirty-six months, most children identify themselves either as male or female. Appropriate sex-role behaviors are taught through reward and punishment. Jeff, in the case study of a prepubescent male in Chapter 3, learned to revere the athletic male stereotype. Throughout childhood he was given gender-specific sports equipment and encouraged to imitate sports heroes. Same-sex adults in his environment reinforced this social learning process until Jeff's identity was shaped to conform to this gender injunction, which created a severe case of role strain. Amelia, also described in Chapter 3, the case study of a Hispanic woman who engaged in role rebellion, also illustrates the process of social learning. She was selectively rewarded and punished until she accepted the female role behaviors her father chose for her.

In both these case studies, free choice did not occur. The individual's gender-based roles, with their attendant behaviors, were externally imposed. The role of biological factors is obscure in both these case studies.

Both males and females can excel in either athletics or academics. Jeff could have become a man without becoming a competitive athlete. Amelia could have become a woman without relinquishing her academic accomplishments. The choices they made were controlled by social learning. Different parents would have shaped different children. Perhaps, if Jeff and Amelia had been taught specifically about the process of learning, they would have recognized the conditioning process and made other choices for themselves about what they wanted to learn.

Can this learning be reversed? Interference with original learning by imposing new learning in the same or similar circumstance has certainly been effective in educational, as well as therapeutic, settings. Both Jeff and Amelia could have been exposed to new learning about sex-role behaviors. Altered experiences presented consistently can modify the impact of early social learning, but this rarely occurs as the segment of the population that presents itself for reeducation or therapeutic intervention is quite small. It is regrettable that the general population does not have the opportunity to modify early social learning should they desire to do so.

Social learning that promotes conformity to sex-role characteristics goes on incessantly. Even after a child becomes an adult, the same messages that shaped childhood development reinforce the learning in the mature individual. The words change, but the message does not. The case of Alice, in Chapter 1, illustrates the mother myth. From the time she was a little girl, she was taught how to be a good woman. When she tired of that role and became aware that she was not known or appreciated as a real person, she gradually stopped practicing the behaviors that the mother role required. Her identity shifted and she no longer defined herself solely as mother or wife. It was a painful shift. Her family punished her. Her son, Tony, withdrew his love, but her family members were not successful in forcing her back into the stereotype. Alice's early gender conditioning had been interrupted and replaced with new learning. This occurred over a relatively short time, particularly in comparison to the length of time it took for her to learn the original mother role. Alice had overlearned the mother role and practiced it far beyond the point of mastery. Perhaps the lack of reinforcement from her family or the community at large for being a mother weakened the role's hold on her. However, it was not extinguished. The guilt, anxiety, and fear she experienced when she departed from the role testify to the strength and pervasiveness of original social learning.

The effects of social influence also operate on a conscious level. Martin, the Gulf War veteran described in Chapter 7, experienced pressure to conform at a conscious level. Direct social pressure was exerted when he attempted to deviate from group norms by resisting combat duty. Both his parents and his girlfriend directly pressured him to comply with group expectations. Martin conformed and later regretted it. The pressure he felt became more severe as the discrepancy between his position and that of the community increased. Martin felt that he was obeying a rule that he objected to on ethical grounds. He became confused and depressed when he betrayed his own value system in favor of that of his community, but the power of social influence was so strong that he could not resist it. If Martin had been educated to understand and anticipate the power of social pressure, he would have been more capable of making a free choice.

Another principle that operates within delusional relationships is the conformation effect. It usually becomes apparent in the reformation process when a negative stereotype has been constructed. When a relationship falters, its counterparts tend to adopt negative views of each other, predicting and noticing negative behaviors in their mates and family members. Even though new behaviors are learned and practiced, the negative view is slow to change. In Chapter 8, Barbara and Claude, the couple reforming their sexual relationship, had developed interconnecting negative stereotypes of one another. They continued to use these negative stereotypes to judge one another even after the offensive behaviors had been eliminated. This occurred because of the confirmation effect, a principle whereby individuals pay more attention to behavior that confirms their existing beliefs than behavior that contradicts it. This is the stuff that social psychology is made of. A knowledge of these facets of social learning would prepare us to make informed choices about our relationships and life decisions.

The negativity bias is another principle what was at work in Barbara and Claude's relationship. Negative traits were weighed more heavily than positive ones. Barbara's negative stereotyping of Claude was more difficult to reverse than a positive stereotype would have been.

In thinking about my work with individuals in delusional relationships, I realize that the lack of knowledge about these principles of psychosocial behavior were contributory factors in virtually every case. Delusional relating was the result of a lack of knowledge. Much of the relating behavior was not consciously determined. Client beliefs about self and others were strongly affected by their past relationships. Impressions of relationship counterparts were manipulated by external forces, often without the awareness of the person being manipulated. Seduction was commonplace. Social pressures operated both directly and indirectly to shape relationship responses.
Relaters were conditioned to assume gender specific roles without regard for their individual differences.

The delusional thinking common in all relationships could be diminished considerably with a knowledge of these basic tenets of social interaction.

Chapter 11

Delusionary Families

You have lived within the confines of your family since birth. It has been your universe, your reference point. You do not recognize the extent to which you have been affected by your family system. You may even think you differ markedly from your parents and siblings. This is not so. All your learning has been filtered through your family's view of the world. Your thoughts, feelings, and behaviors have been judged by their standards and you have judged yourself by their standards. You have absorbed their thoughts, attitudes, and prejudices. You ate, slept, worked, and played in their midst. At some level, you believe that all families are similar to yours. Even though you start to notice differences in high school, it doesn't really dawn on you that there is more than one way to think, see, and hear what is happening around you. The greatest delusion of all is that your family's way of life is the only way of life.

Private family myths bind us just as tightly as those held by the culture at large. Gladys, the daughter of Milton and Sonia described in Chapter 4, is a prime example of how family delusions are transmitted from one generation to the next. The family tradition of wealth and gracious living had been reduced to a symbolic state by the time Gladys reached adolescence. The family myth that poverty was a disgrace was so strong that Gladys could not face the reality of her life without considerable effort to reframe it into a more acceptable form. She researched her family utilizing a geneogram, a chart of extended family relationships, which is used to clarify patterns of behavior. Gladys charted the producers and consumers that had existed in her family. It furnished a structured exploration of her key issues. Eventually, Gladys was able to alter her perception of wealth and status and redefine her position in relationship to work and money. It is significant that Gladys, like so many others, chose to maintain certain aspects of the family myth once she had gained freedom from its hold. Family myths, like cultural ones, promote cohesiveness and stability and can function as either a positive or negative force.

Family secrets, such as the one kept by Stan, described in Chapter 7, have the effect of creating distance and serving as a block to intimacy. When Stan finally told his daughter, Carrie, and wife, Sarah, of his childhood poverty, of which he was ashamed, he released many stored-up feelings that he had experienced and repressed while living in his family of origin. Intergenerational value transmission could not occur in his nuclear family until he had resolved that issue relative to his family of origin. Stan had voluntarily cut himself off emotionally from his parents and siblings because he was ashamed of their social and educational status. The avoidance of emotional involvement with them carried over to his wife and children; something he did not want. Stan felt so deprived of family closeness that he overreacted to his daughter's debunking of his middle class values and feared she would abandon him as he had abandoned his own parents. Carrie's rebellion had an element of projective identification, a defensive mechanism whereby unaccepted feelings of one member are projected onto another. Stan, the father, projected his ambivalence toward his family of origin onto Carrie, his daughter, provoking her to the same behavior. These dynamics operate at a preconscious level. Secrets in families and the heightened emotion they generate fuel delusional thinking. Stan, Sarah, and Carrie were successful in overcoming the effects of this intergenerational pattern of estrangement. This was accomplished by improving their general communication patterns and defusing the impact of family secrets.

Intergenerational loyalties, like other phenomena that contribute to delusional relating, can be either benign or malignant. Judy and Jack, the adult siblings described in Chapter 5 who sought differentiation from their parents and each other, are a case in point. Both struggled to secure a nonnegotiable part of themselves that would remain uninfluenced by other family members. The relationship system, or family of origin, to which they belonged had furnished them with many positive benefits. They were loathe to part with them. This seriously diminished their autonomy and independence. They had difficulty sorting through the duties and obligations owed to parents, siblings, and themselves. Finally, the only way they were able to break the vertical loyalties and establish horizontal ones, with their own mates, was by stealth. Judy literally left town in the middle of the night. Her brother, Jack, was then able to tell his father that he too was leaving. Judy and Jack experienced much guilt and pain differentiating themselves from their family. Although they separated themselves physically, they clearly had not satisfactorily resolved their perceived responsibilities to their parents and each other.

Similar dynamics regarding the discharge of obligations of one generation to another can be seen in the Clayton family described in Chapter 4. On the surface, their dilemma was limited to discharging their obligations surrounding holiday visits of an intergenerational nature. At a deeper level, both parents and adult children were struggling with a maturational crisis. Aging and death were on their minds, but they chose not to acknowledge their deeper-level concerns and feelings. Generally, in a situation of this type, the family map changes and one of the children emerges as a symbolic focal point to take the place of the receding symbolism of the parents. New coalitions and boundaries are then formed, which serve to maintain the structure of the family or origin. In the Clayton family, it appeared that Tina, the oldest child, would assume that role.

Family maps reflect shifts that occur among members at times of death, divorce, marriage, or any significant incident that changes the family's configuration. Ed, the middle-aged male in Chapter 4, who was experiencing a mid-life crisis, totally changed the configuration of his family map: he alienated his two grown children when he remarried a woman over twenty years younger than himself. Ed's children aligned themselves with their mother, Fran, who was dying of cancer. When Ed and his new wife, Grace, had children, the original family structure seemed to dissolve. Fran was too sick and depressed to stand alone as a symbolic focal point of the original nuclear family. This particular family was unable to reestablish a viable family structure, partly because Ed's children from his first marriage were too young to accomplish this on their own. The impact of Ed's delusional relationship with Grace was far-reaching: It resulted in despair and unhappiness for himself and all other members of his original nuclear family.

Divorce does not always alter the family configuration so dramatically. Delusionary relationships are frequently restructured successfully in spite of separation and divorce. In order to appreciate this, one's concept of divorce and family must be expanded to include the relating that occurs between divorced people, particularly when they continue to share responsibility for children.

Delusional relationships do not dissolve with divorce. Sherri and Sam, the divorced couple in Chapter 9, both had substance abuse problems, which they passed along to their daughter, Terri. This was a family that had established a drug-dependent life-style, which was designed to avoid reality. Sherri, the mother, could not face the truth about how she had passed her habit along to her daughter. She continued to use mind altering substances to hide from that truth. Sam, her ex-husband, still symbolized paternal authority to her. When he decided to quit his habit again, it inspired Sherri and her daughter, Terri, to do likewise. Although Sherri did not openly acknowledge that she had modeled drug abuse for her daughter, she changed her behavior in hopes that Terri would follow her example. This actually took place. Change occurred as a result of pressure exerted in therapy. The family continued to be symptomatic, in terms of overused denial and dependence. However, relationship restructuring dissipated the level of delusional thinking that had previously existed.

Comprehensive delusional family systems can be reformed and crisis frequently offers the opportunity. The Watson family, described in Chapter 4, had a secret: the oldest son was gay. They experienced an extreme tragedy when their daughter, Leah, was killed in an automobile accident. Jack chose that time to come out officially to his family. They may have known he was gay and feared he would contact AIDS, but colluding in the family secret allowed them to maintain the delusion. The truth had the opposite effect of what they had expected: It strengthened, rather than weakened, the family and the members reformed their relationships, integrating reality and truth. A dramatic change occurred in their communication system, not just verbally but emotionally, as well. The secret had inhibited them and acted as a barrier to intimacy. Their closeness increased as the delusional system faded.

All families are delusional in that they share in the collection of myths, symbols, stereotypes, and cultural injunctions that permeate the culture in which they are embedded. Each family selects and draws into its system personalized versions of the stereotypes, cultural injunctions, and other elements from which delusions are formed. In Martin's family (Chapter 7), conscientious objection to military service was seen as cowardice. His girlfriend, Delores, came from a family that shared that same opinion: Men went to war to protect hearth and home or they were cowards. In other families, however, going to war and participating in killing could represent the betrayal of a family value, while still others, succumbing to community pressure might be seen as a betrayal of the family system.

There are numerous ways to interpret each stereotype and each cultural injunction. Family systems generally have their own view of cultural prescriptions. Within the family system, individual members may differ markedly from one another in their interpretation of a particular family value. Generally, there are more similarities than differences. Perhaps because each family member has been exposed repeatedly to their own family dogma, a consensual view emerges that differentiates each family from all others in some unique form. This uniqueness forms the basis for family solidarity and delusion.

Mildred's family (Chapter 9) disapproved, but did not actively reject her, when she married an Afro-American. She betrayed a family value, unspoken though it was, when she entered into a biracial marriage, which is still uncommon in the larger culture. The family could not cast her out: that was against family values; however, they could not accept her marriage to a black man. The family had no solution for this dilemma. Their presence in the family session held in my office symbolized family solidarity. They could not resolve the current crisis, but they could reaffirm family loyalty and cohesiveness.

The delusion in this family was that no member broke a family rule. The family rule that Mildred broke was unspoken: no one in the family had ever married a person of color and no one was expected to do so. Everyone had assumed she would not, could not go against the family injunction against biracial marriage, but she did, and its impact on the family was profound. It was now crystal-clear that family rules could be broken, and the entire family structure was thus threatened. The delusion of the family's invincible power over its members was disallowed. Thereafter, a new view of the family had to be constructed. Another delusion could take its place or a realistic view of family power could emerge.

The Jason family had a problem: one of the three sons was disabled. Vince, the youngest son, had been injured in a boating accident when he was four. He suffered a severe blow to the head that resulted in brain damage. Vince had a bubbling personality prior to the injury. He was very happy and loving, and a joy to have around. After the accident, however, there was a dramatic shift. He seemed like a totally different child: he lost his sparkle, seemed withdrawn and morose, and even hostile at times. He seemed to have forgotten much of what he had learned. This transformation appalled his family. His parents were unable to accept what had happened to Vince. They pretended that he would get well and everything would be the same. His brothers, Lee and Pat, didn't like to be around him, but their parents insisted that they include Vince in all their activities since it was hard for him to make friends. At ten, Lee was a shy, nervous child who had a hard time adjusting socially. Vince was a terrible burden to him. Pat, who was two years younger, was fairly popular and did not seem to mind having Vince around, although he frequently got into fights at school with anyone who called Vince retarded or made fun of him. Pat would resort to physical violence. On one such occasion when Pat was fighting with a boy who had called Vince names, Vince wandered off and was missing for about forty minutes. The parents were alarmed and blamed Pat. The teacher on yard duty also blamed Pat, who was suspended from school for three days.

It was at this point that the family entered counseling. During our first meeting I was struck with how confused all members of the family appeared. Vince, the child who had the static dementia, was a little quieter and more withdrawn than the others. The boys moved around a lot and the parents seemed restless, shifting and changing positions in their chairs. It was as if they all had a bad case of the jitters. I pointed that out: "You all seem so anxious. Is it always this tense at home?" They all stopped moving. I felt like I was dealing with an undifferentiated ego mass rather than a family of five separate people.

The father spoke, "It never used to be, but ever since Vince . . . ever since the accident . . ." He couldn't go on--but there were no tears, although there was a heavy sense of gloom pervading the atmosphere. The mother spoke, trying to finish her husband's sentence: "We've never gotten over it. It's as if he . . ."-- she stopped talking.

At this point the room became electric with anxiety. I looked at their faces: again, they seemed emotionally fused. Breaking my rule of silence in cases of extreme anxiety, I asked, "As if he died?" ending with a questioning inflection in my voice. There were sighs, movement, and finally tears, first from Pat and then from the parents and Lee. Only Vince did not cry. He didn't understand or he was too clouded by his impairment to respond. However, the rest of the family grieved. It was long overdue: The accident had occurred a year and a half ago, yet they had not mourned the loss of Vince as they knew him. They were so grateful that he lived that they felt too guilty to mourn the passing of his previous identity. They didn't know how to cope with it the situation: There was no stereotype for this type of situation. They could have more easily handled death, which is more commonplace. This loss taxed the family's identi- ty. They remained suspended, as if in time, stuck together emotionally unable to grieve because Vince was not dead, only disabled. To grieve would have felt disloyal, as if they wished him dead, which they did at times, with each of them silently wishing that Vince, and the family, could have been spared the ongoing grief of his impairment and subsequent limitations.

When I finished the sentence for them with the words "as if he died," I released them from suspension and allowed them to face their truth. The repressed feelings flooded forth. I had no idea when I uttered those words of the magical impact that would follow. I knew only that it would help them work through their grief to face it. I didn't realize at the time that they had been waiting for over a year for the opportunity to grieve and restructure the family identity to include the altered Vince. After that, they were able to differentiate themselves and reassume their own separate identities within the family structure. Realistic reformation had occurred.

MY FAMILY SAVINGS HABITS

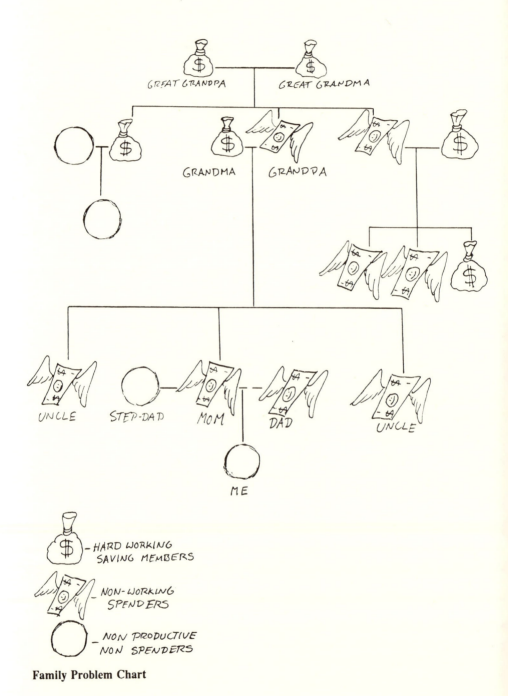

Family Problem Chart

Chapter 12

Restructuring Your Own Relationship

You are in a significant relationship that means a great deal to you. It is not a healthy relationship. You are ashamed of some of your relationship behaviors, but you don't like to admit you are wrong, especially since it gives your relationship counterpart ammunition to use against you. You know you have to get past this fear and your false pride to restructure your relationship. If you don't act soon, your relationship may fail entirely. It has been faltering for a long time. You wish your relationship counterpart would make the first move, but this may not happen. In fact, you may not get any cooperation at all. You're not sure how to proceed. You have decided against professional consultation at this time. It is too expensive and you're a little bit afraid of the counseling process. You decide to follow the process presented in this book and restructure your relationship on your own.

This exploration of delusional relationships has equipped you to evaluate and restructure your own relationships. Scattered throughout the pages of this volume, you have encountered studies of people and life circumstances that may parallel those in your own life. The issues of relationship formation and relationship disturbance are universal, so is delusional thinking. The choice to restructure a failing relationship or abandon it is as profound a decision as any we make in our lifetime. Before abandoning a relationship, attempt to restructure it. You will gain important knowledge about yourself that you will continue to use in other relationships.

It is through relating that we learn about ourselves. If we fear and avoid self knowledge, we relate in a delusional manner. Observing and listening to our relationship counterparts provides valuable information about how we are experienced by others. During a relationship disturbance it is common to avoid listening or seeing ourselves as we really are. Stating your feelings in an appropriate manner and seeking to hear and understand the feelings of your relationship counterpart dispels delusion. If you are in a relationship with someone who prefers delusion to reality, you still have options to make changes in your own relating style. Communication of feelings provides a valuable reality check. Relationship disturbance abounds with misunderstanding. It is not just what you are arguing about, but how you argue. It is common to speculate erroneously about what the other person is feeling, and adjust your relationship behaviors to fit that erroneous speculation.

Doris and her mother had a volatile relationship. They enjoyed one another's company, but after spending an hour or two together, their tempers would flare. Doris's mother, Tilly, had developed the habit of helping her daughter by reordering and cleaning her linen closets. When Doris folded and put away her towels, and sheets, she was usually in a hurry. Consequently, the closet wasn't very tidy. Tilly would refold the towels, sheets and pillow cases, telling herself she was doing something nice for her daughter. Doris resented this but hesitated to say anything because she didn't want to start an argument. She avoided her mother's visits just so she wouldn't have to deal with the closet-cleaning issue. Tilly felt hurt and angry. She was unwelcome in her daughter's home and did not know why.

After attending one of my relationship workshops and telling me that her mother was one of those people who will not change, Doris made a list of her feelings and reactions toward her mother. She also decided how she wanted to approach the subject. She wanted to avoid a fight. She called her mother and they met on neutral ground, at a neighborhood McDonalds. Fifteen minutes into the conversation, Tilly became extremely upset and walked out. Doris had informed her mother that she felt belittled each time her mother cleaned her closets. She felt as if her mother was telling her that she couldn't measure up. Tilly became defensive when she heard this. She recognized that she was being critical of her daughter in an indirect way, but she wanted Doris to be a better housekeeper. Tilly felt Doris's housekeeping skills were a direct reflection on her. If her daughter did not keep her closets tidy, it must mean that her mother hadn't trained her properly. Tilly wasn't sure how she had come to feel so overly responsible for Doris but she had, and it certainly affected her behavior.

Now, she was too embarrassed to admit she was wrong, so she got angry and walked out instead.

Later, she apologized to Doris and told her how it hurt that she was unwelcome in her daughter's house. This interaction was the beginning of their relationship reformation. Both started to think more about what they said and did to one another, and they were pleasantly surprised to learn how much the other valued the relationship.

Had they sought counseling, they would have been guided to improve their communication process by listening to one another's feelings and reflecting those feelings back. The reflection process ensures the accurate transmission and reception of information. They would also have been encouraged to persist or try again after a rupture in communication had occurred. Patterns of relating that have taken years to form do not yield to a single effort to change. Doris persisted in her efforts to communicate with her mother, even after the scene in McDonalds.

When Tilly overcame her false pride and apologized, it divested the relationship of much of its adversarial tone. She was then able to tell her daughter how hurt she was about not being welcome in her home. The two continued to talk, gradually getting to know each other as adults. Tilly had been afraid to let go of her mother role with Doris, fearing they would no longer have a basis for relating. Doris needed her mother's approval of her as an adult woman and was oversensitive to any sign of disapproval or criticism from her.

The initial confrontation had yielded positive results, even though it had been painful for both mother and daughter. Both parties worked at maintaining contact and resolving their mutual issues. What really happened is that Doris told her mother the truth about how she felt, which allowed Tilly to share her own feelings. Neither stopped trying, in spite of difficult moments. A simple, but significant process. Once feelings are ventilated, solutions can be sought and agreed upon. Doris and her mother did not need professional assistance. Reworking their relationship required commitment and persistence. Doris utilized some of the knowledge she had gleaned from attending my relationship workshop. You have been exposed to similar material in reading this book. It is time to apply what you have learned. In order to restructure a current relationship without professional assistance, let's review the restructuring process. This is what is needed:

Acceptance that your current relationship style is delusional. You may not be seeing yourself or your relationship counterpart accurately. Many of your behaviors are the result of preconscious shaping that must be brought to conscious awareness. This involves looking at your current relationship and how you behave in it.

You will need a willingness to face the truth about yourself and relationship counterparts. The commitment to look at the forces that have shaped your relating behaviors is not enough, you must learn to evaluate yourself realistically. Ask yourself, "What is it like to be in a relationship with me?"

Begin to gather information by observing your behavior in relationships. How do you express feelings? How much of yourself do you conceal? When you do withhold information about yourself, what are you trying to accomplish? Learn to distinguish between anger and hurt. How do you act when you are angry, and how does it affect your relationship? Write down the answers to these questions. Then talk about your findings with associates who know you well and solicit their input.

Review this material when a relationship disturbance occurs. This will increase your awareness and decrease the incidents of impulsive acting out behavior which disturb relationships. If you can distinguish between anger and hurt, you can learn to separate them. Hurt can then be discussed more easily. Anger is frequently a reaction to hurt. Ask your relationship counterpart to follow the same procedure. Limit these restructuring sessions to forty minutes twice a week, or at most, every other day. Avoid all-night marathons or extended sessions.

You will want to identify the role models that have contributed to your relating style. Remember that a great deal of learning occurs at a preconscious level. You do not always consciously choose role models, nor do you have the opportunity to select the behaviors that you want to incorporate into yourself from those models. Imitation occurs automatically. This means you have incorporated behaviors into yourself that conscious choice would have disallowed. Look at opposite-sex models as well as same sex models in your early childhood environment. Little girls pick up their father's or brother's behaviors as well as those of their mother and sisters. The same is obviously true for little boys. Cross-gender modeling is common. After identifying your role models, or their absence in your life, take some time to reflect on what you have learned. If possible, talk about this information with your relationship counterpart. Before going on to the next step, make a list of the role models who have figured largely in your life. Clarify what specific behaviors you have taken from them, then decide if you want to affirm those behaviors in yourself or disallow them.

It is also necessary to clarify what stereotypes have affected your development. Remember that a stereotype is a pre-existing mental image that refers to qualities and characteristics of a particular group. It relates to a general, rather than a specific, type. You may see yourself or others in your family as particular types, such as male chauvinist or sensitive male, dumb broad or assertive woman. It is necessary to identify what specific attributes compose your version of a particular stereotype. Determine whether you are in a relationship with someone who can be stereotypically described. Then look closely, both in yourself and in your relationship counterparts, for characteristics that do not fit the stereotype. Upon close examination, resemblances to stereotypes tend to evaporate and a very different person can be identified. No one truly fits the stereotype as each person has unique qualities. Go through this process with each person you have typecast, including yourself. Notice how the generalities do not hold up under scrutiny. Pause again in the information gathering process. Think about what you have learned. Then apply this process carefully to the relationship you wish to restructure. Talk about your insights and reactions, but avoid a prolonged focus on relationship reformation or you will grow tired of the endeavor. Talking about it more than twice a week will belabor the process and make it less effective.

Explore your family history. Look for special family traits and characteristics, and pay close attention to the relating style of family members. List family problems and determine how frequently those problems occur. Be sure to look at communication patterns, family secrets, and symbols. This step takes time. You may want to look at family pictures and memorabilia to stimulate your memories. Conversations with family members about these topics are extremely beneficial.

Conduct a family value search. Ask your relationship counterpart to do the same. What values have been transmitted from one generation to the next? Money, sexual prowess, hard work, good looks, education, having a good time: any or all of these can be family values that affect your view of life and expectations of others. Determine how these family values have affected you and your current relationships. Your relationship counterpart may have conflicting family values and expectations, which have clashed with yours and caused a disturbance.

Ideally, restructuring a relationship involves the participation of all parties. Your relationship counterpart may refuse to participate in this process. You can proceed on your own, increasing your awareness and knowledge base regarding the nature of relationships. At some point, you will make a decision either to remain in the relationship without actively participating in the delusion, or acknowledge failure and terminate the relationship. Your relating skills will have been strengthened by the process and you will be better able to form a healthier, nondelusional relationship with someone else.

If you must terminate a relationship, allow yourself to grieve. Avoid deluding yourself that a magical transformation will occur: it is unlikely. Spontaneous recovery does not apply to delusional relationships: content yourself with the knowledge that you have faced the truth and attempted to reform the relationship. The rest is out of your control. Do not, however, give up easily. Persistence correlates highly with success.

Several years ago, I received a series of letters from a former client, Cloe, describing the process she experienced while restructuring her marital relationship. She and her husband, Max, had separated after their business had failed. Max had been unable to find a job, partially because he did not want to work for anyone else and partially because the economy was poor. Cloe lost respect for Max and blamed the business failure on him. She herself took no responsibility, even though she had functioned as business manager of the card and gift shop they had owned.

Cloe was able to procure employment immediately after they had to declare bankruptcy. She didn't want to support Max on her salary since she believed he simply didn't want to work, so she moved into her own apartment and left Max to flounder on his own. He ended up moving in with his brother and sister-in-law, who owned an apartment building. They gave Max a small efficiency apartment in return for his services as an apartment manager.

Max and Cloe had seen me only once, in a crisis session just before they declared bankruptcy. Both were angry and scared. Cloe was particularly vindictive. In one interchange, she attacked Max for being incompetent and ruining her life: "I should never have married you. My mother was right. You will never amount to anything, but you're not going to drag me down any further." Max did not respond verbally, but tears rolled down his face. Cloe continued: "You've lost everything I had. That was my money, not yours, that went down the tubes because of your laziness." Max closed his eyes. I looked at Cloe, shook my head, and before she could continue, I asked her a question: "Do you want him to answer you?" Her mouth dropped and she stared at me, trying to decide how to respond. Should she continue to attack Max or shift her line of fire to me? She decided to resume her attack on Max. Perhaps I looked like a more formidable opponent than he did. She wanted to fight, but did not want opposition. She seemed afraid of it.

Looking at Max, she said: "Look at you. You're such a wimp. I can't stand the sight of you." I wanted to interrupt her harangue. My first effort hadn't worked, so I tried again. Looking at Cloe, I said, "You must be hurting terribly inside." Cloe stopped. She wasn't expecting empathy and it made her cry. Tears replaced her angry words. Max looked up. He moved closer to Cloe on the couch, but did not touch her, nor did he speak. He looked like a frightened animal.

I explained that they were in shock and that it would take a while for them to return to their previous level of coping. This seemed to reduce their shame, something they both seemed to feel because they had failed in business, and perhaps in marriage. We identified situational supports for both of them, people who could function as temporary care givers since they could not do that for each other. When they left my office, they both seemed calmer. The main decision they had made was to separate, as being together was too painful. As a result of their shame, which they were trying to assimilate, they could not relate effectively. They argued constantly, perhaps to distract themselves from their pain and anguish.

About ten days later, I received my first letter from Cloe:

Dr. Doyle,

I want you to know that I don't appreciate your taking Max's side. You don't know what it is like to live with him. But you were right about my feelings. I'm hurt, not just mad. I guess I get it from my mother; she screamed the loudest when she hurt the most. Not a very good way to communicate. But better than Max; he just sulks or cries. I'm enclosing twenty dollars on our balance. Max will pay you next month. I've only seen him once since our meeting. We didn't have much to say, but at least we didn't argue. We can't afford to see you, so I don't know what will happen.

C.

I was surprised that she had written. I think she needed to feel connected during this time of transition. I sent her a receipt and a folder with handouts from a relationship workshop that I had recently presented. Three weeks later, I got a letter from Max.

Dear Doctor Doyle,

Thank you for everything. Cloe and I are doing better. We get together a couple times a week to do our homework. We both agree that I did not have a male role model, so that's why I'm not much of a man. But I do a lot of other things right. Cloe can't cook as well as I can, so in some ways we are even. But we aren't making it sexually, she won't have anything to do with me. I don't turn her on; she says it's because I'm not man enough. I've got to go now. Maintaining these apartments keeps me busy. Sorry I can't send you any money this month. Things are still tight.

Sincerely,

Max

It was clear that Cloe and Max were dealing with the issue of stereotypes and how their expectations had been shaped by them. I didn't hear from them again for two months, at which time I received the remaining seventy dollars they owed for their crisis session. Cloe also included this chart:

All women in my family are angry, pessimistic, and hard to get along with. They blame others for their own shortcomings.   CLOE   MOM   GMA

The men in my family have no opinions. They keep their mouths shut to stay out of trouble.   MAX   DAD   GPA

I could see that they had worked on the chart together. It was not what I considered a family chart, but it clearly had meaning for them. They also included a list of family symbols and secrets which seemed to have contributed to the delusion in their relationship.

Silence symbolized power and control in their marriage. Max had the power because he remained silent and did not share his feelings. Cloe tried to undermine his power by attacking him and forcing a response, which would symbolize victory for her. Even in the most difficult time of crisis in my office, when Cloe was venting her anger and abusing him verbally, Max did not yield. It was a terrible experience for him. He was afraid of losing control and yielding his power to Cloe.

In their homework sessions, he told her how he wanted to scream back, to defend himself. But that was not the male role, as he had learned it. So he remained silent. His tears and body language revealed the anguish within, but he did not speak and he felt pride in himself for maintaining that position. When Cloe understood what his behaviors meant to him, she regained some respect for

Max. Gradually, the couple restructured their relationship. Meeting regularly to do their homework, or their version of what I had written about in my handouts.

They never came back for another session, but I did receive a card from them when they were at Disney World for a holiday weekend.

Dear Dr. Doyle,
    We made it, and it didn't cost us another $90.00!
                                        Cloe & Max

Not all relationships make it. It takes commitment and a willingness to delve into the forces that have shaped your relating behaviors. Cloe faced an unpleasant truth about herself and the women in her family. She identified family traits that had disturbed relationships for generations. She was able to modify her behaviors once she understood how she had modeled herself after her mother, who was also the product of early childhood learning. Blaming was not in order since it was no one's fault. Once Cloe's awareness level had increased, she reported that often she would stop herself in mid-sentence when she was engaging in one of the old destructive behaviors. She felt pride in her growing self-awareness. As she developed a new pattern of communication, she noticed a significant change in Max. He, too, was reworking his communication style. After making the chart, he started wanting to be his own person. He did not want to continue in a mindless imitation of his father's behaviors, so he started sharing his opinions--slowly at first, but as he became accustomed to speaking his mind, he enjoyed the feeling of freedom it gave him. Cloe was fascinated by the change. It gave her an opportunity to listen and she also found Max more interesting to be with. She no longer felt she had to fight for a response. Together they achieved a more balanced communication system.

Restructuring a relationship can go on for years. Patterns developed throughout childhood and confirmed in adolescence and adulthood do not yield easily to a single intervention. New learning experiences, however, eventually interfere with old learning. This facilitates the establishment of new patterns.

As you increase your awareness and self-knowledge, you will recognize delusionary thinking in yourself and your relationship counterparts. Throughout the restructuring process, you will experience strong feelings: anger, shame, guilt, regret, and fear, as well as joy and pride in yourself for encountering the truth and seeking reality. Many of these feelings will be heavily charged with associations from the past. This means that you will overreact to relationship disturbances in the present if they resemble disturbed experiences you have had in the past. You may often misperceive incidents in the present, assuming they are more similar to past incidents than they really are.

Christopher had an erectile dysfunction. It was not based on any underlying physical cause. He felt insecure in his masculine identity. His wife, Beth, was very understanding. They bought a few books on self-treatment and followed the recommendations closely with success. In less than three months, Christopher's erections were firmer and their sexual encounters had improved. Everything was going well until Beth joined a health club and started to work out regularly. Christopher sometimes joined her but she was more faithful in working out than he was. She also made friends with other club members, including several males. Every once in a while, Beth would stay late at the club. Christopher became suspicious, and one evening when she was particularly late, he drove to the club. As he entered the parking lot, he saw Beth sitting in her car with a man standing next to her open window talking to her. Christopher assumed the worst--that he had just witnessed a clandestine interlude between his wife and another man. Nothing could have been farther from the truth, but Christopher was having an associational response: his mother had had an affair when he was eleven years old and he remembered how upset his father had been whenever he didn't know where Mom was. There had been times when his father had gotten into his car and gone looking for his mother, who had a pattern of marital infidelity. Beth, however, did not. The man was an acquaintance, the husband of a friend. They were talking about a surprise birthday party that Beth was planning for Christopher. Eventually, a few days later, the couple got the incident straightened out, but not before Christopher had peeled out of the parking lot, leaving Beth and her friend astounded at his behavior.

This type of occurrence is a common relationship disturbance. In some cases, it escalates to the level of divorce. A lot depends on how the relationship counterpart handles it. Beth went home and asked for an explanation of Christopher's behavior. He said he knew she was having an affair because she had been gone from the home more often lately without any logical excuse for her behavior. He also said that he wouldn't stand for it and would get a divorce, as his father had done when his mother cheated on him. Beth was very angry. She felt disrespected. At first she thought a divorce would be a good idea since she didn't want to be married to such a jerk. She later reconsidered and told Christopher the truth about why she had been late that evening and absent from home recently. Christopher felt stupid, but he believed Beth and they were able to reestablish their relationship.

Christopher realized what had happened. He had associated Beth with his mother and made the unfounded assumption that she was being unfaithful, just like Mom. Had he not been so upset when he went looking for Beth, seeing her in the parking lot talking to another man would have seemed quite innocent. The heavily charged emotion he was carrying within his system was left over from the past. Unexpressed anger, along with a sense of betrayal, associated with what his mother had done, came to the surface because there was a vague similarity in the two incidents. Overgeneralized feeling is a major component of associational responses.

Christopher and Beth were able to overcome this disturbance in their relationship because they had previously shared successful problem solving when they worked together to resolve Christopher's erectile dysfunction. Each relationship disturbance offers the challenge of strengthening communication and problem-solving skills. Dispelling delusion and restructuring your relationship promotes deeper love and understanding between you and your counterpart. It is an ongoing process. Your culture, with its lack of appropriate education for living, promotes delusion on a daily basis, but with awareness and increased knowledge, you can establish and maintain healthy relationships.

Chapter 13

Relationship Restructuring
for Professionals

You are a mental health professional who has been trained to help people deal with their relationships. You know about communication patterns and family systems. You know something of delusional thinking and how it affects feelings and behaviors. Concepts such as stereotypes, role taking, and gender restrictions are familiar ones. However, you have realized that you, too, are participating in delusional relationships. As a product of our culture, you have not escaped the conditioning process that has affected your clients. You feel a little sick when you realize you have imposed your own values and biases on some of your clients, perhaps even to the point of damaging them. You vow to avoid doing that in the future.

Restructuring relationships is both challenging and rewarding. Your clients have an opportunity to change their view of themselves as well as their view of their relationship counterparts. This process releases them from preconceived ideas that have created disturbances in their relationships; it involves much more than reframing.

Primary goals include helping your clients determine the extent of delusion in their current relationships. This involves extending their knowledge base to include relationship concepts like stereotypes, roles, gender restrictions, symbols, family systems, family secrets, and communication patterns. Personalizing these concepts is important to help your clients feel their impact in their lives.

It is necessary to maintain focus on relationships. All behavior discussed in session must be related back to the original problem of delusional relationships, how their specific relationships were formed, and how they are faltering and failing. Avoid general discussions that do not relate directly to the topic. Your goal is to guide clients in the restructuring of their relationships. Reeducation is part of this process. No blackboards or tests are necessary. Each client views this material differently. You will make a decision depending on your personal counseling style as to whether to go over the concepts in session or give your clients homework assignments.

Feelings are more important than concepts. A cognitive awareness of the concepts will not bring about therapeutic movement. There must be an emotional component to learning. Ventilation of feelings stored up from the past must be fully accomplished. This can be facilitated by asking your clients to talk about highly charged events. Listen for pauses, changes of subject matter, body language and other indicators of stress. Encourage your clients to go deeper into feelings that they may seek to avoid. Evaluate whether full disclosure of feelings has occurred. You need not always press for total exposure of client feelings. It is necessary, however, to comment on their unwillingness to experience deeper level feelings when it is therapeutically appropriate.

Clients respond well to statements such as, "It really hurts for you to talk about this"; "You seem to be avoiding focusing on this topic because you know it will be painful"; or, more generally: "This is the part that really hurts, but there is no way to avoid it. You must acknowledge and feel your pain before it will dissipate." Encouragement and support will diminish their anxiety.

Relationship therapists frequently have problems allowing their clients to feel pain. If you experience this difficulty, procure the assistance of a supervisor or colleague to aid you in practicing this necessary skill. This deficiency may be out of your awareness. Listening to tapes of your own work will clarify whether your responses evoke cognitive, rather than affective, reactions in your clients. If your client focuses exclusively on feelings, you will need to monitor your responses to evoke a balance between cognition and affect. Frequently, clients must express their feelings before they can think coherently. Direct listening accomplishes this. You listen for feelings rather than content. This sometimes challenges the skills of even seasoned therapists: clients recount so many details of their personal lives that it is tempting to focus on the incidents they are describing, rather than their underlying process. Client feelings and cognitions must be monitored regularly throughout each session. There are important cues that indicate when to advance to the next phase of therapy. This is true of individual, conjoint, or family sessions.

In treating relationships, you gain important knowledge about the system by noticing reaction changes members have to one another. You need not comment on this when it occurs, but there may be a time when therapist comments about their reactions in session to one another can be productive. Be judicious in speaking.

Direct listening can be powerful. Utilize eye contact and body movement to reenforce client exploration of feeling. A light movement or shift in your position can cue your clients that they are wandering off point or not dealing with an aspect of the relationships that will yield results. You can utilize non verbal social cues to guide your clients through their exploration of feelings and thoughts about their relationships. In order to do this effectively, you must have a clear sense of the therapy process that you are engaged in, as well as a firm grasp of where your client is in that process.

The need for rapport is obvious. An open, calm demeanor instills a sense of confidence. Establish clear boundaries that limit speculation about your own personal relationships. This will avoid detraction from client relationship issues.

A clear statement about the process of relationship restructuring must be accomplished so that the clients know where they are going and what they are looking for in the exploration process. Timing is significant. Introduction of cognitive material cannot be effective until current feelings have been thoroughly ventilated. The individual, couple, or family members must be given the opportunity to express and clarify the multitude of feelings they have experienced in their delusionary relationships. During this stage it is also possible to teach communication skills and raise their awareness of their own relationship behaviors. It is contraindicated, however, to focus on teaching communication skills. The clients will learn that through your modeling and the subtle use of nonverbal cues. It is only in the later stage of the relationship reconstruction that practice of communication in session yields lasting results.

Negative feelings must be expressed. Clients should be asked to do so gently. Therapists can use reframing techniques to demonstrate nondestructive expression of negative feelings. This, too, must be reserved for later phases of relationship restructuring or you will run the risk of repressing your client's feelings. Sometimes this has to be done to avoid therapist collusion in abuse between clients in session.

Interruption of abuse that occurs in session can be accomplished by interjecting a question such as, "Do you want a response?" or a comment designed to raise client awareness, "Is this how you usually feel toward your partner?" I used this method to interrupt Cloe's verbal abuse of her husband, Max, in their crisis session (Chapter 12). Permitting one client to abuse another in your presence may give the message that it acceptable behavior.

In listening to your clients, you will notice which feelings are most difficult for them to express. Anger masks many feelings. Expression of anger alone does not lead to ventilation. Therapist comments on feeling expression can guide clients toward deeper exploration of those feelings: "You're making angry sounds, but I sense a deeper emotion, almost as if you want to cry."

Once you have facilitated the expression of immediate feelings, you can proceed to focus on the various stages of relationship restructuring through which you will guide your clients.

Introduce the concepts with which they will be working, such as delusion, stereotype, role, gender restriction, symbols, cultural injunctions, and family systems. No specific chronology is necessary. Use your own judgment as to the order with each new case. Avoid establishing a set pattern for the introduction and exploration of these concepts. Responsivity to the client's needs will facilitate learning. It is, however, extremely important to cover all of these concepts and guide the client in fashioning their own definitions of each one. This is a highly charged process when it is done effectively. Guide clients to understand how to apply these concepts to their own lives. They will use them to retrieve information about their relationships.

Encourage clients to look for stages in their own relationships and identify stereotypes, symbols, and cultural injunctions that affected them in the phases of attraction, formation, faltering, and failure. When they talk about disturbances in their relationship, listen, support, and guide them to clarify communication and behavior patterns that characterize their relationship disturbances. Consistent focus on feelings will enable them to gain insight into the impact feelings have on their behaviors. They will then be empowered to modify those behaviors.

Structured experiences such as making relationship murals depicting family activities (Chapter 8 on Noreen and her family) and family charts tracing family traits (Chapter 12 on Cloe and Max) can be done either in or out of session. Any method designed to focus on the relationship, its dynamics, its strengths and its weakness will promote insight and behavior change.

Delusionary relationships need in depth exploration of past relationship experiences. Material uncovered must be related to the present. Simple leads like, "How do you see that experience affecting you now?" keep the focus on current restructuring. Therapist assumptions regarding client ability to make relevant connections from the past to the present are usually unfounded. Emotionally charged experiences from past relationships are overgeneralized. This means clients need help in separating past experiences with other people from present experience with current relationship counterparts. Counseling leads such as, "How is your husband different from your father?" will assist a client in the process of discrimination. Guiding a client to clarify the differences in themselves in the present from the way they were in the past is another way to foster the discrimination process. "You were a little boy then. You didn't have any power. That is not the case today. You are now a grown man with more power than you had then, but you are seeing yourself through a child's eyes. Try to separate the past from the present."

Delusional relationships are characterized by fuzzy thinking. People often impose what they learned in past relationships on current ones. If past authority figures were domineering and controlling, then current mates may appear more domineering and controlling than they really are due to associational responses. This means that they will overreact to current relationship disturbances that approximate past relationship disturbances. You may choose to tell your clients about associational responses in order to heighten their awareness of that occurrence. This will facilitate adaptation. Or you may choose to guide them away from this tendency by utilizing counseling leads such as: "You may be a little confused about what you mother did in the past and what your girlfriend is doing in the present. Sometimes these prescriptions run together. Try to separate the present from the past."

A note about repetition, it is necessary. your clients have been engaging in delusionary thinking for a long time. A single clarification will not be sufficient to dispel confusion between present and past. Reminders are necessary. First, the main point must be communicated by the therapist: "You are confusing the past with the present and part of our work is to separate them." Once this is understood and absorbed by the client, the therapist can then cue the client with a glance or head movement whenever the client shows evidence of confusing the past with the present in session. This type of client cuing should be reserved for significant occurrences.

Delusional relating yields to increased awareness. When clients talk about how their parents related and the impact it had on them as children, they are more likely to scrutinize their own current behaviors for similar patterns. Therapists guide their clients in pursuing this type of knowledge. Insight is not enough. Once clients have increased awareness of their own relating behaviors, they must restructure a new set of behaviors to replace the old ones. In other cases, clients consciously choose to reestablish the old behaviors more judiciously. The magic is in the process. Clients learn about themselves through evaluating their own relating behaviors. They then have an understanding about how these behaviors affect relationships. Change appears to occur naturally.

What has really happened? The therapist has guided the clients through an information gathering process that has raised their awareness of self and others. Specific information has been introduced to broaden the existing knowledge base regarding relationships.

The client now knows more about stereotypes, symbols, role taking, gender based restrictions, and cultural injunctions, as well as how they have affected their relationship styles. Client feelings about relationships have been thoroughly explored. Ventilation of current feelings occurs consistently throughout the process. Residual feelings from past relationships have been discussed and detoxified. The client has been taught to distinguish past relationship disturbances from current ones.

The therapist has functioned as a guide throughout this process. The next phase, restructuring and consolidation, includes clarification of how the client now sees self and relationship counterparts. It is helpful for the client to identify stereotypes that may no longer govern current relationship thinking and behavior. For example, if a client previously had cast the relationship counterpart in the role of protector and provider and has since taken on that role themselves, this change must be acknowledged, discussed, and integrated. Feelings about the shift in stereotypes and their attendant roles also must be acknowledged and discussed.

Structured experiences can be utilized in this phase of relationship reformation. The compiling of scrapbooks and photograph albums can be very useful at this point. Gladys (Chapter 4), in her research on family values, used family memorabilia to aid her in reframing and consolidating her new view of family values regarding wealth and work.

Directive listening on the part of the therapist will yield evidence of changes that have occurred in client's relating style. Reflection and approval of these changes will reinforce the client and impart a sense of accomplishment and confidence. Prior to termination, a summarization process is in order to ensure that new learning is in place. Asking clients to review the restructuring process provides them with an opportunity to comment on your performance as a therapist. Remember that your relationship with clients is a pivotal one. You are part of their new learning. If they have accepted your guidance and modeled themselves after you in some way, your openness to their feedback may favorably affect their openness to feedback in their subsequent relationships.

Incidental learning occurs in the counseling chamber. Your clients will learn from you as they learned from their parents. Your defenses, mannerisms, and communication style may be incorporated by your clients. Social learning is a continuous process which occurs on a preconscious level. As a therapist, you have a responsibility to avoid contaminating the counseling process.

In my work as a therapist and educator, I have benefited from consistent reevaluation of my own unresolved relationship issues. The case of Judy and Jack (Chapter 5), siblings trying to separate from their parents and establish their own autonomy, paralleled in some ways an ongoing issue in my own life. As a parent of two grown children considering relocation, I could easily have identified with Judy and Jack's parents and contaminated their process of individuation. I do not believe that this occurred. However, I am aware that this case seemed to drag on interminably. I did seek peer supervision, as we all must from time to time, to protect our clients.

One other case bears mention. Pearl, in Chapter 2, was seeking to fulfill a stereotype that I personally feel can be very destructive to women, that of the romantic sex symbol. I did not guide her away from that choice, although I disapproved of it. I, like all culture bearers, have been exposed to cultural injunctions that have biased my attitudes and behaviors. In spite of my training and experience, there are times when I feel the tug of the mainstream culture. At that point, I must pause, reflect on my therapeutic endeavors, and ascertain that they are free of value imposition. I recommend that all therapists who are engaged in dispelling delusion and restructuring relationships monitor themselves consistently.

Chapter 14

Conclusion

We have explored delusions. We have looked at delusional relationships, both consensual and nonconsensual. We have identified significant components of attraction and stereotyping. We have looked into the lives of people struggling with role strain and unrealistic expectations. We have seen some of their relationships falter and fail. We have also seen successful relationship restructuring and the emergence of realistic relationship formation. Finally, we have seen glimmers of the magical influence of truth and its ability to release authenticity.

What can we predict if we give up our delusions and our fantasies? What will happen if we recognize the myths and reject the romanticized versions of relationship exchange? Will all the fun be gone? Will relationship magic dissipate? Will reality be too harsh or, simply, too boring? Or is there something better, more genuine, and more uplifting for us to experience in our relationships?

Most relationships can be reformed. By sifting through the stereotypes and unrealistic expectations of ourselves and others, we learn to isolate the authentic, the fine, the good, and the workable qualities and characteristics and to discard or modify delusions and fantasies. We also learn to understand feelings of attraction and rejection and decide whether to make decisions based on these feelings. If we increase our awareness and knowledge base, we can recognize and counteract messages from the culture that beckon us into stereotypic thinking and mindless role behavior. In learning to appreciate reality in favor of delusion, we can eliminate restless feelings of discontent from our current relationships.

An exiting part of realistic relationship formation is the discovery and exploration of people we think we know. There may be a great deal to discover about our relationship counterparts. Throughout this text, we have seen examples of a phenomena called the cognitive confirmation effect, a faulty process in which we categorize others and divest them of their uniqueness. The bi-racial couple, Mildred and Virgil (Chapter 9), both blocked out the steady stream of information from their families that indicated nonacceptance of their marriage. They wanted to be accepted so badly that they would not acknowledge incoming information to the contrary.

Barbara and Claude, the couple who restructured their sexual relationship (Chapter 8), constructed negative stereotypes of one another and proceeded to screen out any positive information to the contrary. It was only after separation and a subsequent courting period that they successfully reversed this process.

The Watson Family (Chapter 4) struggled to accept a homosexual HIV positive member. At first they could not absorb the reality that one of their members was gay. During their time of crisis, their defenses were not as effective as usual. After the denial stage had dissipated, they slowly acknowledged the truth. Jack was gay, he was HIV positive, and he would die of AIDS. But prior to the crisis, when their defenses were down, the cognitive confirmation effect was in operation.

The cognitive confirmation effect is a categorizing process whereby you blind yourself to all characteristics, qualities, and behaviors that do not meet the stereotype you are currently imposing on yourself and your relationships. The story of Mark and Kelly, our first case study, depicting the forces of attraction, also exemplifies this phenomena (Chapter 1). Mark imposed a stereotype on Kelly: the blond cheerleader type. Kelly imposed a stereotype of hardworking male provider on Mark. They used a rough categorizing process touched off by symbols: Kelly's long blond hair and ready smile and Mark's Porsche and his strong, silent, John Wayne-like behavior. They were both wrong. Their perceptions were delusional. The impressions they formed of one another were also delusional. They both knew enough about image making to promote the desired categorization. They blinded themselves to other qualities and characteristics that belied the stereotypes they were imposing.

There is also a behavioral confirmation effect which is a response to being stereotyped. If we are thought of, and expected to behave like a mindless macho or a dumb broad, we are likely to fulfill that expectation. Molly and Pete, the adolescent couple in Chapter 2, who were caught in the behavioral confirmation effect, acted out their versions of gender-based stereotypes to the point of self destruction. The imposed stereotypes elicited the stereotypic behavior.

But as we become more aware, we begin to see ourselves more clearly as we really are, as unique individuals with the potential for feeling, thinking, and behaving without gender-based role restrictions.

Redefining our roles is an important part of this process. We start by broadening our current roles to include new behaviors. This is the point where role strain usually occurs. We cannot maintain all the behaviors from our old role and accommodate additional behaviors from the new role we seek to integrate. We must let go of some of the old behaviors and be judicious about adding new ones. We alleviate the role strain by prioritizing all our behaviors and responsibilities and eliminating those we have labeled as least significant.

The process will falter if the relationship counterparts are excluded or noncooperative in the prioritizing process. This happened to Tony and Alice, the case study of the mother myth in Chapter 1. When Alice, the mother, decided she could no longer fulfill the mother myth and be a stay-at-home mom, she attempted to broaden her role in the family by getting a job and going back to school. Her family members held tightly to the mother myth and tried to force Alice back into the role. They refused to cooperate and support Alice in developing another facet of her identity. Gradually, she reprioritized her mothering behaviors and responsibilities and departed from that role without their support. The process would have been much more comfortable with informed participation of her family members.

Suzanne and Ted, in Chapter 7, accomplished a satisfactory redefinition of roles. This came after their romantic delusion had faded, causing a temporary lack of sexual desire for one other. This is a case study of a couple who freed their relationship from delusionary expectations and gender-restrictive roles, replacing it with realistic roles and more genuine intimacy.

The final phase of role redefinition involves practice and consolidation. There is a fluidity in this process when it is done successfully. The new role encompasses some of the old behaviors and responsibilities, as well as some of the new ones. Role shock is minimized for relationship counterparts and there is a clear understanding that the newly defined role may also change to accommodate emerging relationship reality. Margaret and David (Chapter 8), in the case study of a lesbian who married a man for cover, illustrates the process of consolidating role redefinition. They loved one another, but it certainly was not in the romanticized, heterosexual pattern found in Suburbia, U.S.A. Their sexual relationship represented a compromise. This case demonstrates the interplay between conflicting role expectations residing in the same individual concurrently. Although Margaret was lesbian, she still had expectations of David that a heterosexual woman would have of her heterosexual mate. She desired to keep him in a male stereotype while she departed from its complimentary female counterpart. He protested. She eventually assumed some of the prescribed behaviors for both genders and David did the same. It was a workable compromise. Both parties agreed to it and both acknowledged that it might not be a permanent arrangement. This type of role flexibility may seem threatening to others who seek more permanence and stability in role taking.

Sandy and Bill, the traditional couple described in Chapter 5, divided their roles and responsibilities along very conventional lines. This was a couple who married young and failed to realize that there were other relationship styles available to them. Dissatisfaction with their roles gave them a vague sense of restlessness. They both felt like failures because they had been unable to comfortably fit the stereotypes. Their relationship, like most relationships, could have been reformed, but their lack of knowledge regarding existing options prevented the necessary redefinition of roles. The first step for them was increased communication. They both acknowledged unhappiness with the status quo. That shared admission increased their intimacy. They were no longer pretending that everything was all right.

Culturally induced delusions can be dissipated by sifting through the stereotypes that have been adopted. Clarifying unrealistic expectations of self and others makes it possible for us to appreciate reality and relate more authentically.

What lies beyond fantasy and delusion? Are they a necessary component for relationship happiness? Do we have to delude ourselves about the people we love in order to maintain that love? While it is true that a pinch of fantasy or a slight tint of rose color can be a delight, it is also true that fantasy and rose colored lenses promote delusion. Throughout our case studies, we have seen how delusions fade, leading to relationship disturbance and failure.

We have also seen how reality can be magical--how facing the truth and accepting it can empower us to dispel delusion and reform our relationships. Stan and Sarah (Chapter 7), the middle-class couple attempting to transmit their values to their teenage daughter Carrie, were unable to do so until Stan told the truth and shared the secret of his past with his wife and daughter. This reduced the barrier to authenticity within the family system. It also motivated Carrie to affirm family values and involve herself emotionally with her parents.

The case study involving successful reformation of a sexual relationship (Chapter 8) is another case in which the truth was magical. Barbara and Claude faced the truth about how they were behaving sexually. This permitted them to dispel the negative stereotypes they had constructed around each other. The restructuring of their relationship occurred after they had both accepted the painful reality about themselves as well as each other. They were empowered by truth and reality.

There is another kind of magic which occurs in those moments when one sees the truth and is motivated to a higher level of behavior. Bob's father (Chapter 3) faced three awesome bikers who had rudely shoved his six-year-old daughter out of a ticket line. He risked a fight, in which he would have been sorely beaten, in order to meet his responsibility as a protector. The bikers participated in that moment of truth. They backed down from their original bullying position when they were confronted by Bob's father, a lone man who was doing the right thing. In that time of silence, when they were making their choice about what to do, they felt respect for his courage and acknowledged it in the simple statement, "Sorry Captain, not looking for trouble." It was a moment of truth-- respect and magic.

All case studies demonstrate the need for educational reform. The people involved needed more knowledge about relationships. Their obvious lack of self-awareness contributed exponentially to relationship disturbance. Current methods of transmitting important information about relationships, role taking stereotypes, and cultural injunctions need restructuring. Basic principles of social psychology, taught in sequential units from the primary grades through high school and college, would have prevented many of the relationship dilemmas illustrated in this volume. With regular evaluation and assessment, we could clarify whether mastery of these significant concepts had occurred. This knowledge is too significant to human happiness to leave to chance. Delusional thinking about self, others, and the process of relating could be avoided through educational reform. Realistic relationship formation and maintenance could then occur. It is through relating to others that we learn to know ourselves.

A personal note about my own delusions. In the preparation of this manuscript, I have encountered truth. I have scrutinized my relationships and found ample evidence of misperception, half truths and stereotypic expectation. In seeking to divest myself of this unwanted burden, I have met with a reasonable amount of success. It has been painful, at times extremely so. I have discovered that it is worth any amount of discomfort and anguish to achieve freedom from delusion. I hope to maintain this process of discovery all my life.

Glossary

These terms are defined according to the meaning ascribed to them in this book.

Anxiety disorder. Continual anxiety, reaction to more than one circumstance or event.

Associational responses. An over-charged reaction to an event in the present that at resembles a past incident. Present-time event evokes unresolved feelings attached to the past incident and associates them with the present. The response can occur in relation to people, places, smells, colors, sounds--or any form of stimuli.

Attraction. A piqued interest or arousal response to an individual, usually caused by preconscious, as well as conscious associations.

Avoidance. Psychological defense designed to avoid pain or discomfort. Characterized by changing subject or distracting from painful issues in some way.

Behavioral confirmation effect. A response to being stereotyped. Fulfilling the expectation by engaging in the predicted manner.

Bisexual. Attracted to both sexes. Sexualizes with both males and females.

Bracket. A process whereby feelings in self are acknowledged and set aside so that they do not adversely affect an interpersonal exchange.

Bonding. A process whereby individuals are bound together with ties of emotion and experience. Occurs with repeated common exposure to strong feelings.

Cognitive confirmation effect. A process whereby individuals do not acknowledge behaviors outside the stereotypic categories they have constructed. All else is screened out.

Cognitive dissonance. Discomfort caused by conflict between beliefs, incongruence between new and prior knowledge.

Conditioning. A behavioral term that relates to the shaping of behavior or the process that causes the association of one stimulus with another.

Conformity. Adaptation to prevailing standards or expectations.

Conjoint. Involving two individuals rather than one in a counseling session.

Consensual. Agreement by mutual consent, as in the formation of a mutually agreed upon sexual relationship.

Consolidation. To bring behaviors and ideas together and form them into a solid whole that will maintain its cohesiveness.

Cultural injunctions. Guidelines promulgated by prevailing the culture in both obvious and subtle ways. Directs how to live, look, feel, and be.

Delusion. A persistent false belief.

Delusional relationships. Relationships based on false beliefs, both conscious and unconscious.

Desensitize. To make commonplace so that a startle or shock reaction is no longer evoked, as by talking openly about previously taboo sexual matters.

Erectile dysfunction. Condition wherein the penis cannot maintain sufficient firmness for sexual intercourse.

Exemplification. Assuming a better-than-thou or one-up position, as through martyr behavior.

Family map. Depicts family structure, and can be applied conceptually to nuclear families, family of origin, or extended families. The family map delineates boundaries and coalitions, and can also include family problems and values.

Family myths. A family illusion in which all members collude in maintaining. These myths involve guidelines for behaviors and feelings, and serves to maintain cohesiveness and stability.

Family of origin. The family in which one is born or reared. The roles played within the original family are usually reenacted in some way in the nuclear family. Unresolved issues from family of origin surface in subsequent relationships.

Family rules. Guidelines and rules regarding behaviors, thoughts, and feelings. These are unique in each family.

Family secrets. Under-the-surface, unarticulated information concerning persons or events that are significant to the family history. These may also be private secrets known to only select family members.

Fantasy. An unreal mental image that cannot be replicated in real life.

Fetish. An intense recurrent sexual urge connected with a nonliving object. Items of underclothing are common fetishes.

Gender. Anatomical biological determinant of sex, based on the genitalia.

Genealogical chart. Shows intergenerational family traits or problems in the extended family, and can take on any theme, such as substance abuse, aggression, or sleepwalking. The genealogical chart is more specific than a genogram.

Genogram. A diagram of extended family relationships going back at least three generations. The focus is on data gathering and promotes insight regarding intergenerational patterns.

Heterosexual.   Cross-gender sexual orientation: includes sexual desires and activities.

Homework sessions.   Assignments of educational and therapeutic tasks to be accomplished outside of the therapy session.

Homosexual. Same-gender sexual orientation: includes sexual desires and activities.

Identified patient.   The particular bearer of symptoms in a family or dyad. The individual who is labeled as sick.

Imitation.   The adoption of a particular behavior as a direct result of perceiving another person engaging in that behavior.

Impression management.   A manipulation of another person's impression or attitude through the use of a pose, attitude, or other behavior.

Individuation. The developmental act of separating self from family.

Ingratiation.   A method of impression management accomplished through the use of compliments and giftgiving.

Inhibited male orgasm. Recurrent delay or absence or orgasm in a male.

Inhibited sexual excitement. Recurrent delay or absence of sexual arousal.

Intergenerational.   Across generational or multigenerational lines: for example, involving a child, parent, and grandparent.

Magic. Change that occurs in relationships after the truth is acknowledged, articulated, and accepted.

Magnified differences.   An occurrence in relationships whereby differences between relationship counterparts are perceived to be greater than they actually are due to and attached emotional charge.

Marathon.   An extended counseling or communication session of long duration, (contraindicated in relationship restructuring).

Minnesota Multiphasic Personality Inventory (MMPI). A self-report test designed to measure all important phases of personality.

Mismatches.   Occurs when a person is forced into a stereotype that does not fit the individual's natural tendencies.

Modeling.   To offer oneself as a pattern for others to copy. Can be done with or without awareness on the part of the model (or modeler).

Mystification. The act of mystifying reality so as to obscure it.

Myth. An ill-founded group belief, that is held uncritically.

Negativity bias. A tendency to weigh negative information more heavily than positive information.

Nonconsensual relationship.   Relationships formed without mutual consent such as in a parent-child, sibling, in-law, and business relationships.

Overgeneralization.   A nonspecific response, responding to a broad rather than a specific stimulus, as in making a similar response to all members in a family rather than making individualized responses.

Paradoxical intent. Use of a statement designed to manipulate a response by delivering contradictory messages. A therapeutic intervention designed to evoke the opposite behavior. Reverse psychology.

Preconscious. Used to describe impulses and feelings that lie beneath conscious awareness.

Projective identification. A collusive act between members of a family, business associates, or group whereby aspects of one personality are projected onto and accepted by another member, who incorporates the projected attribute.

Proscription. An imposed restraint or limitation brought to bear on a person or group by a larger entity such as a family, or business.

Rationalization. A defensive phenomena whereby a credible explanation is substituted for an unacceptable action or motivation.

Reality. The state of being real, the absence of delusion and myth.

Reflecting. To give back with the purpose of casting light on the meaning of a thought or feeling. Can be applied to content to aid clarification.

Reframing. A counseling intervention. Challenging existing perception by labeling the behavior differently, thus altering the context in which it is perceived.

Regress. To revert to a younger or less mature level, as when an adult regresses to the level of a child and behaves in an immature manner.

Reinforcement. To reward with the effect of strengthening a response, to increase the likelihood that a given response will reoccur.

Role behavior. Behavior assigned to a particular role, as in provider or protector behaviors, which are traditionally assigned to males. Similarly, nurturing behavior is traditionally assigned to females. In reality, however, such behaviors are not restricted to either gender.

Role models. Persons who serve as patterns for particular roles: for example, mothers or older sisters frequently serve as role models for young females.

Role rebellion. Reaction against the restrictions, expectations, or limitations imposed by a particular role.

Role strain. Anxiety caused by feelings of inadequacy regarding a particular role that an individual is expected to fill.

Role taking. Assuming the behaviors, attitudes, and identity of a particular role.

Rough approximation. An attempt at fulfilling an expectation that results in a near fit to what is expected or prescribed.

Secondary sex characteristics. The maturation characteristics of both genders that designate the onset of pubescence and includes the growth of pubic hair (both sexes); breast formation, and the onset of menses in the females; a lowering of the voice in males.

Self-Promotion. An external method of managing opinion that involves setting forth one's own positive characteristics and omitting the negative.

Shaping. Producing a desired behavior through gradual formation. Behavior for mation is accomplished through repetition and reinforcement.

Static dementia. Mental deterioration that is not expected to remit or improve in any appreciable manner.

Stereotypes. A mental image conforming to a fixed or general pattern, such as an over simplified picture of all members of a particular group. An uncritical expectation of a person, group, or event.

Stereotypic counterparts. The corresponding or opposing member in a pair of general mental images such as Tarzan and Jane, or the dolls, Barbie and Ken.

Subliminal association. Associations of low intensity that are perceived below the threshold of consciousness.

Supplication. A method of external opinion management. Assuming a lowlier-than-thou position.

Symbols. A visible sign that stands for something that cannot be seen; usually chosen by reason of association.

V codes of the Diagnostic and Statistical Manual of Mental Disorders (DSM-IV). A classification of conditions that affect mental health and which do not represent an underlying mental disorder. Listed in the *Diagnostic and Statistical Manual of Mental Disorders*, these codes include marital and academic problems.

Wish Fulfillment. Attainment of an unconscious striving to satisfy a persistent or urgent need.

Selected Bibliography

Ajzen, I., and Fishbein, M. *Understanding Attitudes and Predicting Social Behavior.* Englewood Cliffs, NJ: Prentice-Hall, 1980.

Allen, V. L. "Situational Factors in Conformity." In L. Berkowitz, ed., *Advances in Experimental Social Psychology*, vol. 2. New York: Academic Press, 1960.

Allgeier, E. R., and McCormick, N. B. *Changing Boundaries: Gender Roles and Sexual Behavior.* Palo Alto, CA: Mayfield Publishing Co. 1983.

Allport, G. W. "The Historical Background of Social Psychology." In G. Lindzey and E. Aronson, eds, *Handbook of Social Psychology*, vol. 1. New York: Random House, 1968.

Archer, S. L. "Gender Differences in Identity Development: Issues of Process, Domain and Timing." *Journal of Adolescence* 12 (1989): 117-138.

Atkinson, J., and Huston, T. "Sex Role Orientation and Division of Labor in Early Marriage." *Journal of Personality and Social Psychology* 46 (1984): 333-345.

Bandura, A. "Social Learning Theory of Identificatory Processes." In D. A. Goslin, ed., *Handbook of Socialization Theory and Research.* Chicago: Rand McNally, 1968.

Bandura, A. *Social Learning Theory.* Englewood Cliffs, NJ: Prentice-Hall, 1977.

Bandura, A., and Walters, R. H. *Social Learning and Personality Development.* New York: Holt, Rinehart and Winston, 1963.

Bidwell, R. J., and Deisher, R. W. "Adolescent Sexuality: Current Issues." *Pediatric Annals* 20, no. 6 (June 1991): 293-302.

Bowen, M. *Family Therapy in Clinical Practice.* New York: Aronson, 1978.

Bradley, S. J., and Zucker, K. J. "Gender Identity Disorder and Psychosexual Problems in Children and Adolescents." *Canadian Journal of Psychiatry* 35 (Aug. 1990): 477-486.

Brooker, C. "A Hindrance to Care?" *Nursing Times* 89, no. 6 (Feb. 1993): 34-38.

Broverman, I., et al. "Sex Role Stereotypes: A Current Appraisal." *Journal of Social Issues* 24 (1972): 59-78.

Cade-Haber, L. "The Effect of Employment on the Relationship between Gender-Role Preference and Self-Esteem in Married Women." *Journal of Advanced Nursing* 16, (1991): 606-613.

Carter, D. B., and Patterson, C. J. "Sex Roles as Social Conventions: The Development of Children's Conceptions of Sex-Role Stereotypes." *Developmental Psychology* 18 (1982): 812-824.

Chapman, L., and Chapman, J. "Illusory Correlations as an Obstacle to the Use of Valid Psychodiagnostic Signs." *Journal of Abnormal Psychology* 74 (1969): 271-280.

Chodorow, N. "Family Structure and Feminine Personality." in M. Z. Rosaldo and L. Lamphere, eds., *Women, Culture and Society*. Stanford, CA: Stanford University Press, 1974.

Chodorow, N. *The Reproduction of Mothering: Psychoanalysis and the Sociology of Gender*. Los Angeles, CA: University of California Press, 1978.

Chodorow, N. *Feminism and Psychoanalytic Theory*. New Haven, CT: Yale University Press, 1989.

Cohen, C. E. "Person Categories and Social Perception: Testing Some Boundaries of the Processing Effects of Prior Knowledge." *Journal of Personality and Social Psychology* 40 (1981): 441-452.

Cohen, Y. "Gender Identity Conflicts in Adolescents as Motivation for Suicide." *Adolescence* 26, no. 101 (Spring 1991): 19-26.

Craik, F. I. M., and Lockhart, R. S. "Levels of Processing: A Framework for Memory Research." *Journal of Verbal Learning and Verbal Behavior* 11 (1972): 671-684.

Davis, Dona L. "George Beard and Lydia Pinkham: Gender, Class, and Nerves in Late 19th Century America." *Health Care For Women International* 10, no. 2 (1989): 93-114.

Deaux, K. "Sex Differences," In T. Blass, ed., *Personality Variables in Social Behavior*. Hillsdale, NJ: Erlbaum, 1978.

Deaux, K., and Emswiller, T., "Explanations of Successful Performance on Sex-Linked Tasks: What Is Skill for the Male Is Luck for the Female." *Journal of Personality and Social Psychology* 29 (1974): 80-95.

Diagnostic and Statistical Manual of Mental Disorders. 4th Ed. (DSM-IV). Washington, D.C.: American Psychiatric Association, 1994.

Elaugh, C., Collins, G., and Gerson, A. "Reinforcement of Sex-Typed Behaviors of Two-Year-Old Children in a Nursery School Setting." *Developmental Psychology* 11 (1975): 255.

Fagot, B. I., and Hagen, R. "Observations of Parent Reactions to Sex-Stereotyped Behaviors: Age and Sex Effects." *Child Development* 62 (1991): 617-628.

Ferreira, A. "Family Myths and Homeostasis." *Archives of General Psychiatry* 9 (1963): 457-463.

Firman, D. M. "Comparison of Gender and Victim Response to Violence in Popular Movies." *Health Care for Women International* 12 (1991): 457-464.

Flax, J. *Thinking Fragments: Psychoanalysis, Feminism, and Post-modernism in the Contemporary West*. Berkeley: University of California Press, 1989.

Forehand, R., and Neighbors, B., and Wierson, M. "The Transition to Adolescence: The Role of Gender and Stress in Problem Behavior and Competence." *Journal of Child Psychology and Psychiatry* 32, no. 6 (1991): 929-937.

Galambos, N. L., and Almeida, D. M., and Petersen, A. C. "Masculinity, Femininity, and Sex Role Attitudes in Early Adolescence: Exploring Gender Intensification." *Child Development* 61 (1990): 1905-1914.

Gilligan, C. *In a Different Voice: Psychological Theory and Women's Development*. Cambridge, MA: Harvard University Press, 1982.

Glanz, D., Ganong, L. and Coleman, M. "Client Gender, Diagnosis, and the Family Structure." *Western Journal of Nursing Research* 11, no. 6 (December 1989): 726-735.

Goldner, V., Penn, P., Sheinberg, M., and Walker, G. "Love and Violence: Gender Paradoxes in Volatile Attachments." *Family Process* 29, no. 4 (Dec. 1990): 343-364.

Good, G. E., and Mintz, L. B. "Gender Role Conflict and Depression in College Men: Evidence for Compounded Risk." *Journal of Counseling and Development* 69 (1990): 17-21.

Gutherie, E. R. *The Psychology of Learning*. Magnolia, MA: Peter Smith, 1952.

Haber, C. H. "The Psychoanalytic Treatment of a Preschool Boy with a Gender Identity Disorder." *Journal of the American Psychoanalytic Association* 39, no. 1 (1991): 107-129.

Hall, W. A. "Comparison of the Experience of Women and Men in Dual-Earner Families following the Birth of Their First Infant." *Image: Journal of Nursing Scholarship* 24, no. 1 (1992): 33-38.

Herdt, G. H. "The Development of Masculinity: A Cross-Cultural Contribution." *Journal of American Psychoanalytic Association* 30 (1982): 29-61.

Kohlberg, L. "Stage and Sequence: The Cognitive-Developmental Approach to Socialization." In D. S. Golin, ed., *Handbook of Socialization and Research*. Chicago: Rand McNally, 1969.

Lipsius, S. H. "Normal Sexual Development of Children: Physician Roles in Bridging the Gaps in Parent-Child Communication." *Maryland Medical Journal* 41, no. 5 (1992): 401-405.

Macaulay, R. K. "The Myth of Female Superiority In Language. *Journal of Child Language* 5 (1977): 353-363.

Maccoby, E. E. "Gender and Relationships: A Developmental Account." *American Psychologist* 45, no. 4 (1990): 513-520.

Maccoby, E. E., and Jacklin, C. N. "What We Know and What We Don't Know About Sex Differences." *Psychology Today* 19 (1974): 109-112.

McDonald, D. D., and Bridge, R. G. "Gender Stereotyping and Nursing Care." *Research in Nursing and Health* 14 (1991): 373-378.

McHale, S. M., Bartko, W. T., Crouter, A. C., Perry-Jenkins, M.   "Children's Housework and Psychosocial Functioning: The Mediating Effects of Parents' Sex-Role Behaviors and Attitudes." *Child Development* 61 (1990): 1413-1426.

MacKinnon, C. *Toward a Feminist Theory of State.* Cambridge, MA: Harvard University Press, 1982.

Mead, B. J. and Ignico, A. A. "Children's Gender-Typed Perceptions of Physical Activity: Consequences and Implications." *Perceptual and Motor Skills* 75 (1992): 1035-1042.

Money, J., and Erhardt, A. *Man and Woman, Boy and Girl.* Baltimore, MD: Johns Hopkins University Press, 1972.

Money, J., Hampson, J. G., and Hampson, J. L. "Sexual Incongruities and Psychopathology: The Evidence of Human Hermaphroditism." *Bulletin of Johns Hopkins Hospital* 98 (1965): 43-57.

Moreland, R. L., and Zajonc, R. B. "Exposure Effects in Person Perception: Familiarity, Similarity, and Attraction." *Journal of Experimental and Social Psychology* 18 (1982): 395-418.

Napholz, L. "The Relationship between Locus of Control, Instrumental and Expressive Traits among Nurses." *Journal of Advanced Nursing* 17 (1992): 975-982.

O'Connor, R. D. "Modification of Social Withdrawal through Symbolic Modeling." *Journal of Applied Behavior Analysis* 2, (1969): 15-22.

Parens, H. "On the Girl's Psychosexual Development: Reconsiderations Suggested from Direct Observation." *Journal of the American Psychoanalytic Association* 38 (1990): 743-772.

Pleck, J. H, and Sawyer, J. *Men and Masculinity.* Englewood Cliffs, NJ: Prentice-Hall, 1974.

Pollack, S., and Gilligan, C. "Images and Violence in Thematic Apperception Test Stories." *Journal of Personality and Social Psychology* 3 (1982): 42-51.

Rallis, S. "I Want to Be a Nurse, Not a Stereotype." *Registered Nursing,* (April 1990): 160.

Rekers, G. A., and Swihart, J. J.   "The Association of Gender Identity Disorder with Parental Separation." *Psychological Reports* 65 (1989): 1272-1274.

Rosenfield, D., Folger, R., and Aldeman, H. F. "When Rewards Reflect Compliance: A Qualification of the Overjustification Effect." *Journal of Personality and Social Psychology* 39 (1980): 368-376.

Sears, D. D. "The Person Positivity Bias." *Journal of Personality and Social Psychology* 44 (1983): 233-250.

Stoller, R. *Sex and Gender.* New York: Science House, 1968.

Stoller, R. *Presentations of Gender.* New Haven, CT: Yale University Press, 1985.

Stoller, R. J. "A Contribution to the Study of Gender Identity." *International Journal of Psycho-Analysis* 45 (1964): 220-226.

Stoudemire, Alan. *Clinical Psychiatry for Medical Students.* 2d ed. Philadelphia, PA: J. B. Lippincott, 1994.

Stoudemire, Alan. *Human Behavior: An Introduction for Medical Students.* J. B. Lippincott Company. Second Edition. (1994).

Taylor, M. C., and Hale, J. A. "Psychological Androgyny: Theories, Methods, and Conclusions." *Psychological Bulletin* 92 (1982): 347-366.

Thomas, S. P. "Gender Differences in Anger Expression: Health Implications." *Research in Nursing & Health.* Vol. 12 (1989): 389-398.

Tomlinson-Keasey, C. *Child Development.* Homewood, IL: Dorsey Press, 1985.

Young, I. "Is Male Gender Identity the Cause of Male Domination?" In J. Treblicot, ed., *Mothering: Essays in Feminist Theory.* Totowa, NJ: Rowman and Allanheld, 1984.

Zera, D. "Coming of Age in a Heterosexist World: The Development of Gay and Lesbian Adolescents." *Adolescence* 27, no. 108 (Winter 1992): 849-854.

Zucker, K. J. "Psychosocial and Erotic Development in Cross-Gender Identified Children." *Canadian Journal of Psychiatry* 35 (August 1990).

Index

About the Author

AVERIL MARIE DOYLE is the Director of Clinical Research and Training at Doyle, Dorlac and Associates, Inc. She is a psychotherapist with over 20 years experience as a relationship specialist. A clinical supervisor for the American Association of Marriage and Family Therapists and the American Association of Sex Educators, Counselors and Therapists, Dr. Doyle has contributed numerous to professional journals. She is the author of *The Sexually Disturbed: Treating Psychosexual Disorders* (Praeger, 1992), and coauthor of *A Guide to Sexual Counseling: A Workbook Approach* (1977).

ISBN 0-275-95010-7

EAN

9 780275 950101

90000>

HARDCOVER BAR CODE